FIVE CENTURIES OF
POLISH POETRY

JERZY PETERKIEWICZ
AND BURNS SINGER

FIVE CENTURIES OF POLISH POETRY

1450-1970

SECOND EDITION
WITH NEW POEMS TRANSLATED
IN COLLABORATION WITH
JON STALLWORTHY

GREENWOOD PRESS, PUBLISHERS
WESTPORT, CONNECTICUT

Library of Congress Cataloging in Publication Data

Pietrkiewicz, Jerzy, comp.
  Five centuries of Polish poetry, 1450-1970.

    Reprint of the 2d ed. published by Oxford University
Press, London and New York.
    1. Polish poetry--Translations into English.
2. English poetry--Translations from Polish. I. Singer,
Burns, joint comp. II. Stallworthy, Jon. III. Title.
[PG7445.E3P53 1979]   891.8'5'1008   79-15485
ISBN 0-313-22014-X

891.85108
P625

This book was first published in 1960 by Martin Secker and
Warburg Ltd., 7 John Street, London W.C. 1

This reprint has been authorized by the Oxford University
Press.

Reprinted in 1979 by Greenwood Press, Inc.
51 Riverside Avenue, Westport, CT 06880

Printed in the United States of America

10 9 8 7 6 5 4 3 2 1

ACKNOWLEDGEMENTS

We wish to express our gratitude to :

Mrs. Maria Bunin-Kasprowicz for permission to print the translations of Kasprowicz's poems;

Mrs. Zofia Chylińska-Leśmian for permission to print the translations of Leśmian's poems;

Mrs. Stefania Tuwim for permission to print the translation of Tuwim's poem;

Mr. Zygmunt Serafinowicz for permission to print the translation of Lechoń's poem.

Our warm thanks are due to Professor W. Weintraub of Harvard University for his kind help in reading the Introduction and Notes in typescript, and to Mr. B. Andrzejewski of the School of Oriental and African Studies for reading the second proofs.

Some of the poems from the Anthology have appeared in *Botteghe Oscure* and *Encounter*, and have been broadcast in the Third Programme of the B.B.C.

The cover photograph shows the Horn of the Wieliczka Salt Miners—a bison's horn set in silver with Hercules as a salt miner, made in Cracow in 1534 and now in the Salt Mines Museum in Wieliczka, near Cracow.

J.P.
B.S.

CONTENTS

INTRODUCTION

I

EACH NATION IS OLDER THAN THE RECORDED FACTS OF ITS history, and each literature is older than its first written documents. A few years ago Poles celebrated their national millennium, which began with the baptism of their country in 966. Yet the Polish state must have come into being much earlier.

The year 966 does, however, concern Poland's destiny in Europe, which the choice of the Roman rite had to a great extent determined, linking her culture and, in particular, her literature with the Latin heritage. The impact of this heritage is now apparent in the Polish vernacular even though it belongs to the Slavonic and not to the Romance group of languages : its syntax, for instance, shows traces of Latin influence and allows the writer to bring out stylistic contrasts without straining the idiom.

One should perhaps not draw general conclusions from the scrappiness of extant Polish mediaeval verse, but the development of the native tradition does seem to have lagged behind the rapid growth of Poland's political power. At the end of the 14th century Polish literature was in its infancy, while the Polish kingdom, as the result of a union with Lithuania, expanded eastwards, well beyond the Dnieper, opening new grounds for the influence of the Polish language. Much more has survived from the period around 1450, and relative though this evidence is, one is justified in making it the beginning of a continuous process in Polish poetry.

During the 16th century the Polish-Lithuanian state was evolving the concept of a republic with an elected king at its head and an increasingly powerful gentry. The Polish language was bound to gain strength and to challenge Latin, its long respected rival. The best poets of the early period faced this rivalry in their own work : they wrote both Polish and Latin verse, their native voice always the stronger and the clearer for it.

Seen against its historical setting Polish poetry is five hundred years younger than the Christian tradition in Poland, though an exception has to be made for the first Polish song, addressed to the Mother of God (*Bogurodzica*).* This litany-like invocation, with a syntax as involved as its rhyme-scheme, may have been composed towards the end of the 13th century, but no matter where we place it in the long gap between the baptism of 966 and the manuscript of 1407 it stands there alone, a monument in the wilderness.

Mediaeval Poland was trampled by Mongol hordes, and other invasions brought more fire and plunder to empty the treasures of monasteries and castles. We need not strain our imagination to describe the losses which the country suffered in this way. The introduction to the selection of Polish mediaeval texts, printed in 1950, reads :

> "some of these texts can never be compared again with their originals, because they are irretrievably lost, turned into ashes by the cruel hand of the occupier after the Warsaw rising".

The author refers to the rising of 1944 and the destruction of the Polish capital by the efficient bearers of *Kultur*. If, therefore, the title of the present book indicates a narrower scope than that of the historical millennium, it does so with some pride. *Five Centuries of Polish Poetry* proclaims the life of a defiant tradition which is still capable of rebirth from the ashes, and its very continuance seems to be a poetic miracle.

II

At this point I should like to introduce a few names before discussing the themes and forms of Polish poetry. By doing so I hope to make the later discussion less abstract. Individuals, after all, create literature, and there is no such thing as collective authorship, even when it is called anonymous.

* Not included in the Anthology.

After the anonymous poets of the 15th century, the first writer who received a paternal halo from the historians of Polish literature was Rej, a Protestant propagandist but also a shrewd observer of social and domestic scenes. His verse debate "between the squire, the bailiff and the parson" (1543) has been accepted as the work marking the boundary of the mediaeval tradition, but in fact it belongs to it in form and content. For the modern reader Rej's debate can often be baffling, especially in those passages where the allegorical teaching through proverbs and examples mingles with a satirist's observation of social detail around him.

Topicality entered Polish verse at the time of the religious controversies and made it didactically noisy. Rej, who loved that noise and bustle, became a paradoxical figure for later generations : the Protestant father of an essentially Catholic literature. But a poet of genius could even then manage to rise above religious or political commitment.

This is true of Kochanowski, the first great literary personality, who altered the native poetic diction and has proved as vital an influence for Polish as Spenser and Shakespeare have been for English letters. Educated in Italy after the fashion of his day, he wrote Horatian lyrics, hymns in the biblical vein and witty epigrammatic verse. But his most original work is the cycle of *Laments* (1580), commemorating the death of his thirty-month-old daughter. Here a deeply personal voice asserts itself against literary conventions and mythological or philosophic allusions, showing up their uselessness. In the 19 poems of the cycle a humanist's conflict with his own precepts of conduct is recorded with all the intimacy of grief and then resolved, characteristically enough, in a mediaeval dream-vision. I know no other 16th-century work which would show the same attitude to experience and the same intellectual honesty in a lyrical statement.

Among the many baroque poets in Poland, two should be singled out, for they have, in my opinion, a timeless quality of wonder which shoots through the trappings of the gilded style. They are Zbigniew Morsztyn (not to be confused with other Morsztyns in 17th-century literature) and Zimorowic, author of *The New Ruthenian Idylls* (1663).

Zbigniew Morsztyn has survived almost by chance, the complete collection of his emblems being published as late as 1954. With other poets of his turbulent age he shared the whims of fate, which caused their works to be known only in manuscript, preserved some of them in private anthologies, and in the end let scholars discover them for our modern taste.

Particular attention should be drawn to the strange religious context of Zbigniew Morsztyn's poetry, which is grounded in the beliefs of the Polish Antitrinitarians (Arians), who have recently become the object of enthusiastic research. The movement, though never large, had a moderate egalitarian orientation and attracted some of the outstanding minds in the country. There is an intellectual restraint and exactitude in Morsztyn's emblems. His language is less conceptual than that of Donne, and avoids on the whole the traps of metaphysical wit. Herbert may be a closer analogy. Morsztyn often builds his ideas on quotations from Solomon's Song, as if to emphasise the loving voice within his verse.

On the surface, Zimorowic seems to be a more glittering poet, a master of extreme moods, using pastoral sweetness as well as macabre fancy. He claimed to have followed the elegant models of the native idyll, but in fact he packed the form with all kinds of subject matter, including realistic war *reportage*, and he did not hesitate to throw in sophisticated remarks about the state of Polish poetry. *The New Ruthenian Idylls* is a singularly rich volume and, because of its complexity, prone to be misunderstood by those who prefer to keep literature in tidy compartments. The date of its publication, 1663, has a historic significance. The idylls appeared in print after the rebellion of the Cossacks (which is described in two horrific pieces of *reportage*) and after the invasion of Poland by the Swedes. How could Zimorowic, a truly regional writer, view the destruction of the Lvov district with pastoral complacency ? Nor could his religious queries come from the depth of tranquillity. He saw terror and beauty in the creation, and like Job heard and asked those huge questions which in themselves were poetic paradoxes.

The baroque style lingered in Poland well into the 18th

century, and, though opposed, it still left some mark even on the younger classicists (e.g. Kniaźnin). One man who freed himself wholly from the impact of the 17th century was Krasicki, a dignitary of the Church and friend of the last king of Poland. He excelled in satire, epigrammatic fables and mock-heroic poems rather than lyrical poetry.

Unlike this sceptical bishop, Karpiński, a poor nobleman from the south-east corner of Poland, wrought a deeper change in the mode of expression by bringing lyrical poetry close to personal experience. The autobiographical core of his work sustained many diverse experiments with form, including the pastoral song. Karpiński had an uncanny gift for adaptation and travesty, and seemed to do these things so effortlessly that his later critics suspected him of facile lyricism. Nothing could be further from the truth, and a poem like *Recollection of Past Love* proves Karpiński to be an intelligent craftsman, capable of an almost modern analysis of emotion.

He belonged to the tragic generation which had to witness the slow murder of their country by Russia, Prussia and Austria ; he lived on after the final partition of Poland (1795) until the year 1825, when the Romantic style he had foreshadowed was given full expression in Malczewski's narrative poem *Maria*. This short tale, idiosyncratic in language and almost cinematic in the sequence of its scenes, unfolds against the melancholy landscape of the Ukraine which seems to absorb, at every turn of the plot, human moods charged with the presentiments of tragedy and crime. Incident and character interact so much more closely than in most Romantic tales that it would be difficult now to treat them as separate parts of a poetic atmosphere.

Mickiewicz and Słowacki are the embodiment of national Romanticism, which can still appeal to the communal feelings of most Poles. Mickiewicz, in particular, exercises this possessive power over them, and no matter how strongly one may resist the bardic claims, there is so much familiar charm in the quotable and over-quoted passages from *Pan Tadeusz* that one's memory warms up and dissolves criticism. A great deal has been written about *Pan Tadeusz* as the last successful epic of European literature, but for non-Poles its regional background (Lithuania) might perhaps seem no less exotic than the circumstances in which the poem came into being. Written by an exile and printed in Paris (1834), this truly national work acquired its Homeric dimensions precisely because it had grown in a foreign environment, each childhood recollection projecting some myth of the lost country.

Like Mickiewicz, Słowacki chose to live in exile after the revolution of 1830, and like Mickiewicz had to expand the images of his childhood and youth to make them last for a lifetime. His chief contribution to literature lies in the poetic drama, although he never saw his plays performed. As a lyrical poet he could often express the dilemma of émigré freedom in a manner devoid of patriotic rhetoric, e.g. in *Hymn* or in *Give me a mile of land*. His mystical poems, on the other hand, show a strange affinity with the poetic diction of the Symbolists.

It is remarkable how much of the topical poetry written by the Polish Romantics has become topical again, on a much wider scale, interpreting from the past our sinister age with its brain-washing, mass deportation and mass murder. *Prisoner's Return* is an extract from a play by Mickiewicz, based on a political trial in Vilna, which for the poet ended in deportation. When read today, this colloquial piece has a double authority, because it speaks for the particular experience and for the fear which is persistently with us. And we find similarly uncomfortable analogies with the present day in Słowacki's poetry.

The obvious weakness of literature in exile arises from its self-centred preoccupation with the function of writing, which is then bound to be elevated to prophetic or mystical heights. One step further, and the writer places himself on an imaginary monument above literature itself, a solitary light *in tenebris*.

Norwid reacted against all this with his ironic probing into the meaning of beauty, work, patriotism and sacrifice. His was the most independent mind in 19th-century Polish poetry, but he also paid for it with poverty, unhappiness and bleak solitude. Ignored by his contemporaries, he was unearthed from oblivion in the beginning of the present century and is now a powerful source of influence, both literary and moral. He can be trusted by those who distrust all kinds of propaganda, for in his own life Norwid refused to be bullied by slogans and sham righteousness, whether political or social, orthodox or progressive.

His contribution to modern poetry, although made a century ago, places him in some ways close to G. M. Hopkins, in others, to Laforgue and Ezra Pound. The full extent of Norwid's originality within the native tradition is hard to grasp, unless one establishes first a critical context for his experimental works, like the verse dialogue *Promethidion* (1851) or the collection of poems *Vade-mecum* (1866). Most of his letters, too, should be treated as artistic concepts, because they mirror a mind that could not stop being creative even as it fought despair.

The first great poet of peasant origin was Kasprowicz, who came at the end of a barren period in Polish poetry and revitalised not only its subject matter, which needed a more direct contact with folklore, but also its form (Norwid's influence had not yet emerged from obscurity). In 1902 Kasprowicz published his first set of hymns which, being rooted in the tradition of penitential songs, expressed what must have been most vivid in the religious imagery of his peasant childhood. Using the technique of association, he introduced other elements and arrived at a musical pattern which was to organise the material of all his longer poems. Free verse helped to shape their structure.

Kasprowicz was a contemporary of Yeats, with whom he shares a tendency towards symbolism, but unlike Yeats he had once been part of a genuine rural culture, for which he needed no substitute later. He could always rely on his ear for popular metres, and when he finally decided to simplify his verse, he transformed the ballad stanza into a highly sophisticated medium for yet another attempt to overhear the whispered soliloquies of God.

Two modern poets can be safely included in this survey without being distorted by some kind of fashionable bias. They are Leśmian, who died in 1937, and Czechowicz, who died in 1939. Both have been revived since, and partly reinterpreted.

Leśmian represents a poetic fusion of the Jewish and Polish heritage; a striking combination when accompanied by linguistic experiment. Leśmian's vocabulary is certainly inventive and abounds in metaphoric turns of idiom ; but at times it seems to lull his verse with lisping evocations of peasant speech. His fantasy, though, has a restless and compulsive rhythm of its own. Crippled creatures invade the glossy wonderland of his meadows and woods, in which sensuous love is often confused with necro-mantic violence. How far can this be related to the shock tech-nique of the Symbolists ? Was the poet's intention to shock, or did he want to deliver himself from the nightmares visiting his words ? An answer should perhaps be sought in poems like *The Cemetery*, where the mood of hopeful resignation shrouds all previous conflicts.

Czechowicz was killed by a German bomb at the age of thirty-six. His poetry illustrates the *avant-garde* movement in Poland, but it also shows an independent imagination at work. This does not mean that Czechowicz rejected or defied the *avant-garde* theory which he had adopted. On the whole he remained faithful to its canons : the primacy of metaphor and free verse. His steady development was due to the understanding of these two precepts, and he died a mature artist.

Czechowicz, however, knew how to cultivate the sources of his imagination and in this respect he acted prudently, like a farmer. His village background was his strength, and he was sparing with the urban motifs fashionable at the time, which he never used merely for their own sake. There is a sense of unity even in his poems of despair, just as there is a strange expiation in his fore-bodings of war crimes. *Grief*, for instance, could be a postscript to our feelings of guilt after the war, but it was written in 1938, a year before Czechowicz's death. He had borne that prophetic guilt in him until it exploded together with the bomb that killed him.

III

Translation removes the barrier of language, but it runs the risk of also removing some of the characteristic features which the original texts possess. Fortunately, a national tradition is not imprinted on the language of texts alone.

Each literature, I think, has its favourite ingredients and these, of course, are used in countless combinations. Their flavour can be recognised under the changing guise of epoch and style—the national dishes continue to be served with subtle self-assurance. I shall attempt here to describe a few recurrent themes and forms which constitute the ingredients of Polish poetry. In the previous section only twelve poets have been introduced, and so once again I am going to restrict myself, assuming—with all due respects to my reader—his unfamiliarity with Polish literature.

During the 16th century, the centre of power in Poland shifted to the landed gentry, and the country squire who had an understanding of literature besides his political and religious interests would quite naturally become a poet in his spare time. Writing for him was a civilised hobby as much as other pastimes suitable to his station. And what could be more appropriate than occasional verse in praise of husbandry and the beauties of village life?

It is true that Rej turned this hobby to a moralistic purpose, but nevertheless he remained all his life a poet squire, depicting in verse and in prose "the life of the upright man", by which he meant, of course, the life of a nobleman in the country. In Kochanowski the moralistic purpose merged with the hobby, and a skilful instrument of art began to shape Polish poetic diction. Yet even he, scholar, courtier and man of some influence, willingly retired to his village. There he extolled its peaceful joys in *The Song of St. John's Eve*, and there he reached a profundity of reflection in the cycle of laments on the death of his daughter Ursula.

Two themes developed out of this conviction that the country was the proper domain of the gentleman and his muse: the first was concerned with the more practical aspects of husbandry, the second favoured lyrical nuances and was closer to the *Eclogues* than to the *Georgics*. Thus both themes drew on the authority of Virgil, and in their development overlapped from time to time, especially when the poets began to play on baroque contrasts.

Yet the lyrical nuances brought in real originality and it is because of them that Polish idylls could in the course of one century become the representative national form. A poet who called himself Simon Simonides launched the idyll in his volume of 1614, for which he provided the native term *sielanka*. In spite of his classicised name, the Polish Simonides made a creative use of the vernacular, and by exploring its idioms, proverbs and rhythms tainted the pastoral convention of Theocritus and Virgil with his own sensitivity.

Within the same volume of twenty idylls, he performed different tasks as an artist : he translated, adapted and reshuffled his classical models and, what is more important, added a few examples himself, among them *The Reapers*, a harvest scene of so authentic an atmosphere that some critics have reduced its meaning to a social protest. The protest, however, is addressed to the sun by a peasant woman who sings it, and on this pagan song the poem's meaning rests. *The Reapers* pointed to new possibilities within the formula, and fifty years later Zimorowic boldly widened the scope of the idyll to include all kinds of experience.

There was, of course, a descriptive type of verse, expressing the poet's satisfaction with rural bliss, which often amounted to mere catalogues of village delights, and these, after all, remain virtually the same. But the idyll did more than this : by avoiding pastoral self-indulgence it could adapt the descriptive method to a criticism of life, which regenerated the form for a long time to come.

In the 18th century, for instance, Karpiński allowed discreet irony to shift the focus of his pastoral songs, and the Romantics who thought of him as their poetic kinsman carried this practice even further. The Polish idyll survived many odd trials of technique during the 19th century, and the process is by no means at a standstill today. The vitality of the idyll, however, is most evident in the beneficial influence it has had on narrative poetry.

Mickiewicz's *Pan Tadeusz* is a good case in point. We know that the poem was conceived as an idyll, but it outgrew its original framework. An essentially humorous vision of life had something to do with this. Again and again Mickiewicz makes us see his pastoral background through the eyes of such characters as the Count, a cranky pursuer of whims, and Telimena, a sophisticated but ageing pursuer of men. Ironic distortions result, giving the story a new depth, and even the heroic theme is partly affected by them. The march of Napoleon's army through

Lithuania thunders in Mickiewicz's verses, but fortunately for the poem the noises of war are kept at a legendary distance, the squire's manor and the countryside remaining the centre of reality.

A travelling hero of one of Słowacki's plays describes St. James's Park as "the enchanting idyll of London". Słowacki himself was a traveller in exile, and the foreign landscapes inspired some of his best poems. *In Switzerland* (1839) is certainly his most successful attempt at integrating scenery and the changing emotions of love into an idyll with an elegiac ending. His idyll recalls, on one level, a mediaeval combat between mundane and divine love, and on another the startling appositions, at which 17th-century pastorals excelled. The loss of innocence is suggested by the parallel changes in the scenery itself, each Alpine image being at once real and symbolic ; and the ending has the elegiac finality of nature's yearly dying.

Here perhaps lies the explanation as to why landscape so often has a functional purpose in Polish (and generally Slavonic) poetry. To put it differently : something which is static as part of a background can also assume an active rôle and become part of a human experience. This two-way traffic between man and nature creates more than just lyrical moods, it creates a reflective condition similar to an intellectual process which transforms our sensations. In the West reflective poetry tends on the whole towards argument, and at its worst is drowned in abstractions. Slavonic poetry, on the other hand, seems to rely almost exclusively on the concrete features of landscape as both receivers and pro-jectors of mood, but at times this double mediacy weakens the structural spine altogether.

Poets with a strong sense of structure like Norwid, exploited the landscape idiom to the full. It was not description for description's sake, but an ultimately ironic way of showing the plans and works of man in their natural setting, landscape being a reminder of the past no less than picturesque ruins. We find a clear example of this in one of Norwid's later poems, entitled *A Dorio ad Phrygium* (1872), which is also his best experiment in free verse. The static permanence of a rural civilisation is the poem's structural focus, attracting towards itself all the scattered relics and symbols of history.

Similarly in Kasprowicz's hymns, which belong to Symbolism proper, the natural images perform a highly functional purpose, endowed with the same magnetic power to attract every other allusion. So active are they at times, that the poet feels compelled to detach them from their roots altogether, and he shows gigantic landscape on the move. This kind of vision, hypnotic and horrific as well, seems a far cry from the serenity of pastoral scenes. But we should not forget that the classical idyll admitted magic and ritual : there are these almost secret links running through the poetry of Theocritus, Virgil and the Polish Simonides, of Zimorowic and Kasprowicz, until they emerge in modern poems such as Czechowicz's *Idyllic Dream* and *Through the Borderlands*.

I have already mentioned that in Mickiewicz's *Pan Tadeusz* pastoral and heroic elements mingle freely, but I have not yet discussed the heroic concepts of Polish poetry. They appeared two centuries before *Pan Tadeusz*, and were influenced by the political problems of the day and by the baroque revival of Lucan. His *Pharsalia* inspired two Polish translators, and by an unhappy coincidence provided a parallel with the civil war in the Ukraine (1648).

Twardowski made a point of calling his huge versified chronicle *The Civil War with the Cossacks, Tartars and Muscovy, then with the Swedes and Hungarians* (published posthumously in 1681). The middle years of the century which he recorded were certainly under the influence of Mars, and there was something epic in the sweep of events that involved great states and nations. The heroic concept, however, depends on the choice of the Enemy, whose grandeur must equal the poem's theme. In a religious epic like that of Milton, Satan is the arch-enemy beyond any parallel, his grandeur for ever resting on the mystery of evil. For the 17th-century Pole there was only one enemy, grand enough and mysterious enough to deserve full epic treatment : the infidel Turk, surrounded by the galaxy of his multinational armies.

With wonder and involuntary respect Potocki described the approach of the Turkish army in his poem *The Chocim War* (written about 1670), and the list of exotic names and places built up the atmosphere of mystery. He could not help turning Sultan Osman into a powerful character : in fact, he bowed before the concept of the great enemy and gave him heroic qualities. Despite its many faults, *The Chocim War* is true to the spirit of the 17th century and contains passages of exceptional merit, especially when the feeling for landscape meets with the epic sense of history.

The proximity of the Islamic world sharpened historical awareness in Poland as it had done earlier in Spain. Analogies between countries are, of course, risky, but Poland does resemble Spain in some of its attitudes, one of them being the heroic concept as expressed in *pundonor*. Different in language and race, these two national traditions mark the boundaries of Europe in a dramatically similar way.

Another characteristic Polish poetry has in common with Spanish is the way in which folklore seems to be lying just under the surface of the accepted norm or convention, and is relatively easy to bring out. Because of this, sophistication ceases to be a distinctive feature of the literary form as opposed to the primitive. Moreover, the further one looks into the past, the harder it is to identify these primitive sources. In the beginning of the 17th century, for example, special collections of Polish songs were printed for the burghers and peasants (e.g. *The Villagers' Kermis*), though the primitive quality of the themes is most elusive. What were they exactly ? And what made Polish carols acquire a rustic flavour so that they are now the peasant's favourite poetry ?

I have selected a few folk-songs for our anthology, and they are, I think, good illustrations of the kind of sophistication we find in Polish poetry as a whole, irrespective of its social origin. My impression is that the same could be said of Spanish popular poetry.

In the light of this observation the success of poets like Karpiński is better understood. His religious songs, for instance, reached all classes of people, partly because they had recaptured the forms familiar from anonymous collections. A hundred years after Karpiński, a poet from Cracow succeeded in producing an unusual drama called *The Wedding*, which he had based on the structure and metre of the puppet Nativity play. The author, Wyspiański, stressed its authenticity by giving away the real identity of his characters. The wedding itself had a model also : the poet confirmed the local reality and then pierced it with the cruel symbols of history and folklore.

What makes *The Wedding* so unusual is its dramatic manner, taken over directly from the puppet theatre, doggerel and all, yet transformed into a personal statement about life, unique and indestructible. Wyspiański was a very uneven writer and his language suffered from fits of eloquence. In *The Wedding*, however, he found the right medium, which could not be used again. Perhaps the end of any sophistication is reached through such an obvious discovery as his : that literature prefers to shift its masks over the surface of life.

IV

I should like to add a few notes on metre and language. But first I ought to state that I agree with those modern authorities who think the Greek metrical terms misleading when applied to post-classical vernacular poetry. Quantity is absent from Polish verse, and in contrast to the function of stress in English, Polish lines have a syllabic basis.* Readers familiar with French verse should rather look there for analogies with Polish, though the commonly used lines in Polish poetry are different again.

The most characteristic line has thirteen syllables with a caesura after the seventh. Its obsessive quality is such that any practitioner of Polish verse hears it echoing in his mind, always ready to oblige him. For this and other reasons the thirteen-syllable line deserves the name of a national metre and can be compared in status with English blank verse and the French alexandrine. Being a standard metre, the Polish line is capable of serving all types of poetry : we find it in the epic and the drama, in reflective and descriptive lyric, in mystical and humorous verse. It also has an ancient lineage, beginning with samples among the

*This does not preclude tonic elements, noticeable especially in Romantic and modern poetry.

first mediaeval poems. Moreover, its high standing was confirmed by the works which have since become national classics. Kochanowski's laments, Simonides's and Zimorowic's idylls, Potocki's epic of the Chocim war, Twardowski's chronicles, most of Krasicki's fables, Malczewski's *Maria*, Mickiewicz's Crimean sonnets and his *Pan Tadeusz*—all these testify to the flexibility and strength of the thirteen-syllable line. Indeed, it would be inconceivable to imagine Polish poetry without it.

Perhaps the next metre in order of importance is the octosyllabic line. Favoured by mediaeval versifiers, it was also chosen by Rej for his debate between the squire, the bailiff and the parson. Later it lingered on in didactic and occasional verse, to be revived by two 19th-century dramatists, Fredro and Słowacki. Fredro made it a brisk volatile medium for dialogue, as in his great comedy *The Revenge* (1834); Słowacki, on the other hand, thought the octosyllabic line the right measure for conveying the Calderonian atmosphere of his mystical dramas.

This line was, of course, associated with the rocking rhythm of doggerel couplets; and so those poets who tried to experiment with popular metres, often used it for a sophisticated purpose. Wyspiański, for instance, based the persistent rhythm of *The Wedding* on the octosyllabic line which he extended and contracted according to the mood of a scene. Kasprowicz, too, allowed this measure to be the backbone of his free verse, and though his hymns did much to bring out the tonic qualities of speech, they nevertheless relied on the traditional syllabic unit which mediaeval prosody had handed down through religious songs.

The combination of lines in stanzaic poems varied from period to period and from poet to poet, but again one can single out types which have had a longer success in the native tradition. The combination of alternating seven-syllable and nine-syllable lines seemed to have established a sort of lyrical convention. Yet the effect of Karpiński's *Recollection of Past Love* depends on the seven-syllable line alone, carried throughout this pastoral song, with the rhymes alternating in the *ab-ab* sequence.

Finally, we have the eleven-syllable line, used by Morsztyn in most of his emblems, and later by Romantic poets. Słowacki exploited its possibilities to the full in his sonorous poems, such as *Hymn* or *Give me a mile of land*, or, to take a more complex example, in his masterpiece *In Switzerland*. The eleven-syllable line has also been accepted as the best metrical equivalent for rendering Shakespeare's blank verse into Polish.

Polish poets have often complained that their language is poor in rhymes, by which they usually mean the shortage of mono-syllabic, i.e. masculine rhymes. Kochanowski was partly respon-sible for ousting mixed rhymes (feminine ones coupled with masculine), which had been the feature of mediaeval verse, but they returned later to help the comic muse. Masculine rhymes by themselves have remained in peasant poetry, and one is not sur-prised to find both Wyspiański and Kasprowicz delighting in their strident sound. Yet, all in all, Polish verse prefers to keep feminine rhymes in a safe majority.

What the Polish language lacks in rhymes is generously com-pensated with the wealth of its vocabulary and syntax. The Latin elements in these are sometimes emphasised to bring out con-trasts, and in the Baroque age this was an obvious stylistic advantage. Zbigniew Morsztyn could thus produce memorable phrases by rhyming words of Latin origin but appropriately fitted with a Polish case-ending. The following lines from *Emblem 51* show just that :

> *Serce do słońca wielką relacyją*
> *Ma, a księżyca mózg influencyją.*

There seems to be a greater mobility in an inflected language, and Polish certainly gives this impression, particularly in poetry. Not only do the aspects of its verbs contribute to a clearer sense of action, but the system of declensions, with its seven cases, also helps to set nouns in motion. A compact poetic sentence in Polish has an almost epigrammatic power of persuasion. On this compactness and persuasion rests the authority of Kochanowski's verse and much of Norwid's hard achievement.

Two further examples should be added to illustrate the poet's taming of syntax. Sęp-Szarzyński, who wrote at the time of Kochanowski, left a group of religious sonnets, in which the precision of thought and feeling seems to have been imprinted on the very shape of each sentence. Similarly, in Krasicki's fables the art of brevity triumphs through the syntax, and there every verbal aspect has a part to play, nailing down the exact meanings of the argument.

Perhaps in the final test, serious poetry proves to be the one which does not compromise with language, either for its merely musical qualities or for a colloquial obviousness of idiom.

V

The anthology presented in this book consists of a hundred poems ; a modest number, but I hope that all of them are good literature. I am entirely responsible for the selection.

Naturally, I have tried to choose texts representative of the literary periods, styles and individual authors, but not, I hope, too conventionally representative, for such texts are often covered with a thin layer of antiquarian dust, or smell of schoolroom appreciation. The reader has, I think, been spared quite a few banalities sanctified by anthologies and should be able to find here at least some fresh air to breathe.

Unavoidably, a number of extracts from longer works had to be included. Without them this book would have become narrowly lyrical and less solid in texture. Some passages therefore come from epic works like *The Chocim War* and *Pan Tadeusz* ; others from plays like *The Ancestors* and *The Wedding*. But each forms a separate unit and can be assessed out of its context. Unfortunately, no extract is given from Słowacki's poem *In Switzerland*, although it is mentioned twice in the introduction. I felt that for structural reasons I could not isolate a lyrical fragment from the whole. All these editorial decisions are stated in my notes at the end of the book. The notes give the original titles as well as essential information about the texts, and a minimum of biographical data. For clarity, a brief entry about each poet comes first, followed by critical comments where necessary, which incorporate biographical detail relevant to the text.

The quality of our translations determines the usefulness of everything else in this book. And here I wish to express my gratitude and admiration for the work of Burns Singer, who produced the final versions of the poems. His firm poetic judgment guided our mutual efforts over those risks and pitfalls which bewilder many a translator. At the beginning of our work we agreed to aim at reproducing the essential features of the selected poems, precisely because we could not assume the reader's familiarity with the Polish literary tradition. This made our collaboration even more arduous and exacting.

It has become fashionable among recent translators to dispense with metrical patterns and rhymes altogether, for the sake (we are told) of clearer meaning. But what is the meaning of a foreign poem denuded of the form which makes it what it is ? We have preferred to be old-fashioned and struggle with complex patterns of form in order to recapture also that part of the original text which had been shaped by poetic diction. For this the technical versatility of Burns Singer was invaluable, offering a range of stylistic equivalents, from mediaeval lyric and baroque conceits to symbolist imagery and peasant couplets.

For nearly two years we prepared the anthology, meeting once a fortnight to discuss and collate the different versions. We share many critical views and our attitude to poetry is basically the same : this, of course, facilitated the initial efforts, and often enough the collaboration looked like a series of tests, confirming our literary beliefs.

During those two memorable years many glasses of wine were emptied to fortify our resolution and to appease the demons of both languages. I hope the wine sacrifice was not in vain.

JERZY PETERKIEWICZ

TRANSLATOR'S PREFACE

POLISH VERSE IS SYLLABIC, WHEREAS ENGLISH IS STRESSED. THIS means that the translator is faced with similar problems to those which confront the translator from French into English. The repeated failure of those whom I would not dare to attempt to emulate in the writing of English syllabic verse discouraged me from attempting to bring English into line with Polish practice. Instead, I have tried to find equivalent English metres for the large range of Polish ones which are covered in the present anthology. Thus the classical Polish line of thirteen syllables has been translated throughout into pentameters. This has led to an apparent lack of logicality since there is also a Polish line of eleven syllables which could be transferred into nothing shorter than a pentameter. To avoid this confusion, however, would have meant committing the thirteen-syllable line to the mercies of the English alexandrine than which there is no more uncertain vehicle in our language. It therefore seemed better to use the pentameter for both the eleven- and the thirteen-syllable lines.

Again, Polish rhymes are, in general, feminine, and masculine rhymes tend to sound queer or plain funny, as do feminine rhymes in English. This left the way open to a simple substitution of masculine rhymes for feminine ones, and vice-versa. While, however, it would be true to say that every masculine rhyme in the pages that follow has a feminine equivalent in Polish, there are a number of feminine rhymes which have feminine counterparts in the original. In rhyming, then, as in everything else, the prime consideration in my mind was the integrity of the poem as a work in English verse.

A few words would seem appropriate about the method by which the present work was composed. Since I myself have no knowledge of the Polish tongue I had to rely entirely on the literal versions given me by Dr. Peterkiewicz. These versions would be given me at fortnightly intervals, accompanied by notes on the characteristics of the verse, and I would retire with them to emerge a fortnight later with draft translations. Dr. Peterkiewicz would then suggest minor alterations in order to eliminate my misinterpretations of his text and so the present versions were hammered out in an atmosphere of complete cooperation, with consultations at every phase of the process.

Some poems fell very naturally into English, others were more difficult and some proved completely impossible. One strange fact emerged : that the poems with which I had least sympathy often came out best. For example, I found myself violently opposed to the whining tones of self-pity in Juliusz Słowacki's *Hymn*, yet once the original refrain had been changed from "Lord, I am sad", to "Master, my heart is sore", the whole poem fell easily into its present shape. Some of the poems which I instantly liked, those of Kochanowski and Kasprowicz in particular, gave me many anxious moments, and I must admit that I remain unsatisfied with my versions of Kochanowski's elegies to his daughter.

Finally I should like to express my gratitude to Dr. Peterkiewicz for having introduced me to the magnificent literature of his native land. For two full years now my head has been ringing with Polish names : Krasicki, Karpiński, Norwid, Tuwim, and, continually, I have been surprised by the degree to which these odd-sounding characters have expressed sentiments so intimately connected with my own life. I can think of few ways in which I could have been more profitably employed, and none more pleasurably, than in the composition of the present book, breaking, as it does, one more of the barriers which language puts between one man and another and which keep in silence, as far as our ears are concerned, many of the mightiest of human voices.

BURNS SINGER

POSTSCRIPT 1970

My collaborator, Burns Singer, died suddenly in 1964, four years after the publication of *Five Centuries of Polish Poetry*. Except for a few corrected misprints, this new edition preserves the original version of the book which has become for me a memorial to a long and inspired friendship.

Seven more recent poems, however, have been added to bring the anthology up to date, all of them translated in collaboration with Jon Stallworthy. I feel very fortunate that a poet of his subtlety and accomplishment was willing to continue the work of Burns Singer and he has, in my opinion, succeeded admirably.

The principle determining the choice of these supplementary authors was the same as for the whole selection : no living poet has been included. I believe that the biographical fact of death allows for a view above the current exaggerations of fashion. A more detached assessment is at least possible. For it is the contemporary section in many a comprehensive anthology that baffles after a lapse of time. The reader has then to brave the last pages, the *pons asinorum* of what once seemed durably safe. I stand by my principle because in a book of this scope, no matter how limited its number of pages, centuries must be balanced against one another.

Is death, however, a meaningful selector? It seems to be for eastern Europe today, where some ironies of fate can only be uncensored by death. A note on Broniewski's poem (p. 136) testifies to this : it could not have been written while he was still alive. Even within the range of these seven tests, the characteristic voices of modern Polish poetry speak out against the complex mood of a country which has no longer any use for self-pity. Prison, mental illness, journey towards entrapment : these are the themes. Yet Bąk lifts his song "above madness". There is a mature quality of experience at the core of these poems ; Broniewski and Piętak, for instance, hold on to some faint shadow of faith, although they see themselves exposed to doubt and derision.

A few of the poets who are now writing (Grochowiak, Herbert, Karpowicz, for example) have had their verse translated into German or English, but if one wishes to show the full map of recent Polish poetry, writers of peasant origin, like Ożóg, deserve much more attention. I do not want to apply social bias, I am only stating my belief : the village heritage has a redemptive quality for Polish culture in this age. And it is not a coincidence that Piętak's poems, nurtured by this heritage, should end the anthology.

JERZY PETERKIEWICZ

ANONYMOUS (c. 1450)

Lament of Our Lady under the Cross

Hear me, my dears, this bleeding head
I want to lament before you turn ;
listen to this affliction that
befell me on Good Friday.

Pity me, all of you, old and young,
The feast of blood will be my song.
I had a single son,
it is for him I weep.

A poor woman, I was rudely confused
when I saw my birthright in bitter blood.
Dreadful the moment and bloody the hour
when I saw the infidel Jew
beat and torment my beloved son.

Oh, son, sweet and singled-out,
share your pain with your mother.
I carried you near my heart, dear son.
I served you faithfully.
Speak to your mother. Console my great grief
now that you leave me and all my hopes.

Small boy, if you were only lower
I could give you a little help.
Your head hangs crooked : I would support it,
your dear blood flows ; I would wipe it off.
And now you ask for a drink and a drink I would give you,
but I cannot reach your holy body.

Oh, angel Gabriel
where is that range of joy
you promised me would never change ?
You said : "Virgin, you are filled with love,"
but now I am full of a great grief.
My body has rotted inside me and my bones moulder.

Oh, all you wistful mothers, implore God
that such a sight may never visit your children,
not this which I, a poor woman, now witness,
not this which happens to my dearest son,
who suffers pain and yet is guiltless.

I have no other, I shall have no other one,
only *you*, stretched on the cross, whom I call my son.

ANONYMOUS (15th Century)

From earthly decay

From earthly decay the soul flew away :
In a green meadow it went astray :
Weeping in sorrow, its thoughts were not gay.
Saint Peter came and said :
"Why are you here, weeping in sorrow ?"
The soul replied :
"Since I don't know which way to go
I stand quite still, weeping in sorrow."
Saint Peter whispered :
"Soul, sweet soul,
Come to the Heavenly Kingdom. Rise.
I'll take you into Paradise."

ANONYMOUS (15th Century)

Charm

Rosie, rosaiden : there were three maidens.
Our Lady, Mary, walked on the sea and plucked a garland of gold
foam.
And then Saint John came down and asked : "Where are you
walking, my dear ?"
"I'm off to cure my son."

Mikołaj REJ (1505–1569)

Indulgences

So the fences crack and break
When they crowd festive for their soul's sake.
The priest in church shouts and shrieks,
The churchyard barrel crackles and leaks.
Someone shakes a wicker basket ;
Another a drum, a pipe or a casket ;
While the third cranes his neck up
To shout to the cantor or drain his cup.
And they count eggs—the hens shriek
On the altar—the pigs squeak.
And truly indulgences came our way
After we'd squeaked our brains away.
And yet King David did the same
When, on his harp, he praised God's name.
They go away believing twice
That they have gained by sacrifice.
And certainly their throats are filled.
If that's reward they should be thrilled.
Few of them remain alive
Till hours for evening prayers arrive.
By vesper time there's many a neck
Ploughs the ground on a long trek.
They carry him to the fence by the head.
"Indulgences were too much," it is said.

4

Jan KOCHANOWSKI (1530–1584)

Song

What do you want of us, great God, who gives
Limitless favour to each thing that lives ?
The Church will not contain you, you, entire
In every inch of water, land and fire.

Riches is useless since to you alone
Belongs each jewel that man thinks his own.
A grateful heart, great God, is all that can
Be offered to you by poor things like man.

You built the sky, embroidered galaxies
And sketched foundations so that from them rise
Perimeters too huge for men to trace :
Earth's nakedness you covered with green grace.

Great God of all the world, the sea obeys
Your vast commands and keeps to its set ways.
The rivers richen. Day knows when to dawn.
Night and the twilight linger and are gone.

The Spring brings garlands and the Summer wears
A crown of wheat like girls who dance at fairs.
Autumn dispenses apples, wine and mirth.
Then winter sluggishly prepares the earth.

At night your gardeners spray each plant with dew.
By day your rain wakes withering plants anew.
The beasts eat at your hand and every sense
Is nourished by you with munificence.

Immortal God, grace most continual,
Be praised for ever. Keep us where we shall
Best serve your purpose, now and when we die
Safe in the shadow of your wings that fly.

5

Lament VIII

This house grows very empty now you've gone
My dearest Ursula, and there is not one
Among the many who remain with me
Who can replace your vanished soul ; or free
Us from the misery of your absent song,
Your talks and jokes that got the facts all wrong.
You hid in corners and your mother smiled.
You tugged your father's sleeve and so beguiled
Him from the thoughts that soured his bit of brain.
You laughed as you embraced them both again.
But now you're silent and these empty rooms
Hold nothing playful to dispose their glooms.
Our sorrows squat in corners : and delight
Is what we search for vainly, day and night.

Lament X

My gracious Ursula, I have lost you. Where ?
In which direction ? in what land ? what air ?
The lesser angels, are you with their hosts ?
Or are you one of Charon's weeping ghosts ?
Are you in Heaven ? or on the Happy Isles ?
Or does pale Lethe wash away your smiles ?
Or are you feathered and your song as clear
As is the nightingale's ? O, have you shed
Your maiden graces now that you are dead ?
Or do some sins remain from human clay ?
Does Purgatory singe those sins away ?
Have you regained the home you had before
Your birth rejoiced my heart or made it sore ?
If you exist at all, pity my grief.
And, if you cannot come, for my relief,
Back in your proper shape, then as pure soul,
Mere shade, substanceless nightmare, come, console.

6

In Defence of Drunkards

Earth, that drinks rain, refreshes the trees :
Oceans drink rivers : stars quaff up the seas :
So why should they make such a terrible fuss
Over insignificant tipplers like us ?

To A Mathematician

He discovered the age of the sun and he knows
Just why the wrong or the right wind blows.
He has looked at each nook of the ocean's floor
But he doesn't see that his wife is a whore.

Mikołaj SĘP-SZARZYŃSKI (c. 1550–1581)

On these words of Job:
Homo natus de muliere, brevi vivens tempore etc.

Man, birthed in shame, lives very painfully,
Briefly in change, his state on earth, and knows
He, like a shadow, fearful as he grows,
Will perish abandoned by the sun, and die.

And yet, O God, within yourself most high,
At one with what you are, whose glory flows
Endless and happy—you, for praise, impose
Your greed on us, nor human love deny.

Your charity is strange : the Cherubim,
A chasm of understanding, wonders : and
To Seraphim the righteous flame shines dim
Although they burn by it, love's brightest brand.

Most holy Lord, let us possess no more
Than you would give us and we can restore.

SĘP-SZARZYŃSKI

On the War we wage against Satan, the World and the Body

Peace would make happy : under the heavens though
We fight our life. He who commands the night
Wages cruel war ; and vanities delight
In quickening our corruption with their show.

And there is more, O Lord, that you must know :
Our home, this body, greedy, fleeting, bright,
Heedlessly envious of the spirit's might,
Continually covets endless woe.

Weak, careless and divided, what can I,
Engaged in all this combat, gain alone ?
O universal King, O peace most high,
Your mercy is my hope, or I have none.

Let me come close, Lord, teach me what to do,
Then I shall fight them and, thus saved, win through.

Simon SIMONIDES (1558–1629)

Pietrucha's Song to the Sun

The steward's coming back. I'd better try
To sing for him and make his face less wry.
His whip is ready. We have much to fear.
But he likes songs : see, he inclines his ear.
"Sweet eye of day, small sun, pure light and true,
Please teach our steward how to be like you.
You brighten day with beams, but still you share
Your power, leaving black night in the moon's care,
Since you know nothing lives alone in heaven.
O may he take the example you have given.
Our steward should be wed. You have the moon
Who keeps the music of the spheres in tune.
Sweet eye of day, small sun, pure light and true,
Please teach our steward how to be like you.
You climb the skies : the silver stars retreat.
The moon comes up : they kneel down at her feet.
And so in homes. Though masters keep their powers,
Servants obey the mistress, as we would ours.
If he would only wed, our steward could
Expect us to remain with him for good.
The manor gates would yawn to let us in.
Long days of pleasant pastime would begin.
Sweet eye of day, small sun, pure light and true,
Please teach our steward how to be like you.
You warm us and spread mercies from the sky.
Night is your absence : dawn is your reply.
May he beam down like you and our work be
Finished before the dark falls finally."

Andrzej MORSZTYN (1613 ?–1693)

To St. John the Baptist

Of course you are the messenger, you who
  Shed the grey brightness which the sun breaks through.
As when pale dawn provokes the birds to play
  Their music glorifies the shape of day,
So your birth violates your father's tongue
  Till, from his lips, a shriek of praise is wrung.
And as the sun burns red when the last gleam
  Of styptic dawn admits a blood-red stream,
Your blood, too, gushes on the world whose fate
  The sun you herald will illuminate.

Andrzej MORSZTYN

On Little Flies: A Song

Quite stainless, Kate, and white as frozen snow
Your face still lets these needless freckles grow.
    I admit my hackles rise
    When milk is speckled by such flies.

Bright though you are, you imitate the sun
And blind us also with small spots of dun.
    I lose my tongue and both my eyes
    In gazing at those tiny flies.

And will they hurt us ? At our first embrace
My kisses will disperse them from your face.
    Grant me the least of courtesies,
    My lips will chase away those flies.

O do not spare them from my appetite,
Or you can never know my power aright.
    Thirsty for love, my hunger sighs
    To feed upon those flimsy flies.

Andrzej MORSZTYN

Song

Kate, are you sick or obstinate
    Or angry with the troops ?
Even though the Queen's been here in state
    Your Prettiness never stoops.

It can't be cold that keeps you there :
    The frost won't take the blame.
If you were here, your beauty's flare
    Would set our huts aflame.

Nor should the fusillades alarm
    As some of us suggest.
Caution is needless since no harm
    Can pierce a stony breast.

Besides, for your defence, you train
    A bright artillery.
Grenades explode and bullets rain
    Where'er you cast an eye.

Then, too, your aim is surer than
    Iron's ever is.
You hit the heart of every man,
    Unlike our enemies.

Come, visit me, my little sun.
    Eclipses should be brief.
I am besieged and not Torun.
    You must bring my relief.

Make a covenant with prayers.
    Forsake your nunnery.
Three vespers said, even monks repair
    To join the soldiery.

13

Zbigniew MORSZTYN (1620 ?–1690 ?)

Emblem 39

The Bride came to seek the Bridegroom during
the night, and found him—asleep upon the cross.
Inscription : "By night on my bed I sought him
  whom my soul loveth : I sought him, but I
  found him not."
Solomon's Song, III, 1.

Breathless I run ; all day I've searched this place
Straining my eyes and ears to catch some trace
Of him I love. And then some men reply
That he was seen asleep at home. So I
Enter our house and tiptoe to his door
Afraid to waken him whom I adore.
But he is gone, and where he lay feels chill.
Yes, he has vanished. I search again, until,
Now without hope, at last I see him lie
Without a sheet or pillow, nakedly
Stretched on the cross. His only bedding is
Pain, passion, torment, his death agonies.
O, my Beloved, is this then your room
And your repose ? this cross ? this blood ? this doom ?
Is combat sleep ? a duel where you meet
Death and the devil, promising defeat
Since only then can you my sinful soul
Restore to joy and make my sickness whole,
When, from your death, eternal my salvation
Though, for my sins, endless your mortification.

Zbigniew MORSZTYN

Emblem 51

The universal sphere is revolved by holy love so
that it may become more perfectly spherical.
Inscription : The sphere will be more perfectly a
sphere.

Round universe, where only spheres can range
Though sizes differ amd the colours change :
The sun, the moon, the stars, the heavy earth
That draped itself in oceans at its birth,
Eternal love allows each to possess
All properties of roundness, nothing less.
And this same love winds up the world, its clock,
And teaches months and years the way to walk :
And all for man, for mortal man, because
He is the image of great nature's laws.
Red heart, red sun, but one vast congruence :
The moon exerts her silver influence
Upon his brain. The same occurs in metals ;
In beasts, fish, reptiles ; inhabits trees and petals,
Makes Wildness grow and what is sown by hand.
In ants it happens, instructing them to stand
And walk and run. Yet shadows all of these
To what salvation's holy pure decrees
Has promised men by love which will be given
When they live finally through it in Heaven.

Samuel TWARDOWSKI (1600–1660)

The Sultan at the Mosque

Next day, the Emperor ceremoniously
Feasted in person at the Santa Sophia.
A mob from Asia and another from
Roumelian provinces massed beneath its dome,
Making the Mosque a mask of strange attire.
Tall turbanned heads, bright caftans in the choir,
And togas, silken, shimmering like flame,
Workmanship various as the tongue can name.
Not shapes of sea-shells on a shore of sand,
Their patterns whittled by sly nature's hand,
Nor shades of tulips from a myriad buds
Drowning whole valleys under fragrant floods,
Could more delight. The Emperor sat down,
A silent populace stilled at his frown.
As though pulled tight by one unbroken string
They stood in an impenetrable ring.
The mitred Mufti raised his arm and prayed
In a loud voice. (His stole was pure gold braid.)
The others, as though dumb, prayed silently.
Their foreheads touched the ground obsequiously.
They lay quite prone when they heard Allah's name,
Then knelt when that of their great prophet came.
But, their prayers over, *Halla* was their cry.
The Mosque's floor trembled, and its great domed sky.

Cupid's Suicide

Then, flying from the town,
That stupid child, dimpled with deep renown,
Came to a river banked by graceful trees.
He chose a myrtle from among all these
And hanged himself. The branch above him bent.
The rich cord tightened. Gold-haired and innocent
His head bobbed heavily as a poppy pod
That, wet with rain, leans over towards the sod.
The wind arranged his locks. His nape bowed low.
His eyes, now narrowed, kept their beauteous glow.
But his wings drooped, their colours changed and numbed.
His red lips were by white saliva gummed.
His childish lungs still laboured for their breath.
He kicked the air, just once : and that was death.

But O ! if one of all those ladies who,
Tall and half-legendary, have suffered through
That boy, if one had known what he would do. . . .

Epitaph for a Dog

Your master dead, your life all out of tune,
You, Garsonek, on Thursday, died at noon.
    You'd waited by his coffin for his call.
    Beside his grave you'd watched the damp night fall.
You scented his familiar footsteps and
Followed until, by Charon's cruel command,
    A small beast on no errand, you were tossed
    Overboard whimpering; and the ferry crossed.
You dared not enter Lethe since you had feared
Water during your life : and so you reared
    Back from the bank and barked and whined in vain,
    And ran about and waited, and barked again.
Now you will howl forever on that shore.
Your own death holds you and the water's roar.
    We, to reward the endless love you gave
    Your master, give your corpse an earthen grave.

Wacław POTOCKI (1625–1696)

Winter, before the War

The frost bit deep. When heavy guns were dragged
Across a marsh no inch of bogland sagged.
The dubious fords raised solid crystal beams.
A glass bridge spanned the deeper parts of streams.
The snow was shameless in its secret keeps
Though clouds had dumped it carelessly in heaps ;
But where frost parched it, sparkling silks were spun
And polished lilies to receive the sun.

Someone to whom the war means nothing yet
Glides on a sledge, its runners barely wet,
So light it seems : one horse has leopard spots
And one's hawk-mottled, bird-like as it trots.
A hunter with his hounds treks through the snow.
But, soaking toast in beer by the hearth's glow,
An old man sits. He doesn't want to drive
Off in a sledge. The Spring will soon arrive
And his death with it. Now, since his teeth have gone,
He sucks soaked bread. If any man lives on
Until his youngest grand-daughter gives birth,
This is the last delight he'll find on earth.
In short : the sun reached Capricorn—no more—
And Winter fell from heaven to this hard floor.

The Turkish Army

Those wondrous Negroes massed there, whose white teeth
(Peering with icy brightness from beneath
Black smolten glass, their swollen lips,) would scorch
The eye that watched them as sparks singe a torch.
The Mamelukes, their tunics broad and white,
Scattered through that great field and, like a flight
Of swans above a rookery, banners spread,
Thick Turkish *bunchuks* flapping overhead.
Taurus, rock rope where Hercules won fame,
From both its sides the clambering nations came.
From Carmel where Elijah's prayers brought tears
To heaven's cheek that had been dry three years.
From Calpe's and Abyla's limbs of stone,
And from tall Ossa, once Typhoeus throne,
Whence giants who expelled the gods from heaven.

The Lydians came, Pamphylians, Kurds, and even
Armenians, Myndii, Seres, Macedonians ;
Cyrenaei came, Angorians, Anatolians ;
From Cappadocia, Pontus, and that town
Where sulphur burns and asphalt glue's upthrown,
Sodom, they came : bald-headed Arymfaeans,
Cadurci, Latophagi, Cyrcei, Sabaeans,
Egyptians, Massagetae, Bisalts, Hyrcanians,
Imawi, Bactrians, Phrygians, and Albanians,
Psylli and Pargiotes, Gelonians came :
Ganges, the Nile, and Tigris, lent their name :
From where the Hydra meets the Crocodile,
From Vulcan's Lemnos and from Eden's mile
Where Adam lived who taught mankind to die,
From Memphis, Babylon, Cairo, Tripoli,
From the whole Orient now in decay
They came. Yet from the Danube, nearer they,
Bulgarians came, and Bosnians, men from Thrace,
The Cherkes, Rumi, Silistra, each race. . . .

Bartłomiej ZIMOROWIC (1597–c.1680)

Judgment Day

He will be heard no more : his song
Won't speak to friends he's left behind
Until the trumpet can unwind,
And that trump's reverberation
Penetrates through all creation,
Opens the graves of all the dead,
Wakens us who long since bled
Present for judgment in the form
Perished in ashes, now grown warm.
Death will grieve to understand
And finish itself with its own hand
And those who deal us doles of time
Will bang the earth with their useless chime.
The sun will faint from sudden fear.
The face of the moon will be covered with gore.
Thrown from heaven by foul disease
Terrified stars will fall and freeze.
The earth's foundations will jerk, and rocks
Like sea waves, give each other knocks.
All human craft, all human deeds
Will be burnt up like moorland weeds.
Haughty castles and cities will fall
And worldly pomp find a dusty pall.
Vain things, extravagance, delights
Will disappear under the thickest of nights.
The world will shudder then and wear,
For its own self, its mourning gear.

ZIMOROWIC

Against Bad Versifiers

Brash embryo poets populate our season
So that our language has more verse than reason
And every lout the commonality breeds
Fouls it to satisfy his brutish needs.
The Muses once were sacred and revered
Touched seldom, by such bards as Cyntheus heard.
Now they are common property and wail
Knotted by hands that can't tie a goat's tail.
Poets rape words. With ignorant dissonance
They croak away like magpies on a fence.

Queries

Earth and the whirl of air, the circling sky,
These are my triple texts. They clarify
God's goodness till their living image glows
And I read truth through their three folios.
What spark lights up the sun and makes it burn,
An endless lantern as the years return?
Who drives its flame-maned chargers? And what force
Keeps its bright cart so perfectly on course?
Who costumes night, the youthful prioress
Whose face each evening wears new tenderness?
And why is she not weary with the changes?
Who plants the seeds of dew? And who arranges
For morning to be varnished fresh each day?
Who brightens the extinguished stars which play
Like shy sharp fingers with the hackled snow?
That fleece, what makes it? How do hailstones grow?
And who has pinned upon the wind its wings?
Or given this world so many different things?
Who tells tonight that last night has gone by?
Nor deviates though daylights multiply?
What mind hacks minutes from slow centuries
And documents with clocks what no man sees?
As at a rollcall, the small seconds shout
Their names and hours, and hours take turn about.
And when Favonius chases lazy ice
Far into Tartary, with his winged device,
The melting snow beyond Hercynian shores
Grumbles and crumbles almost as it snores;
And youthful Spring unsheets her gentle bed
And rubs her cheeks with dew till they shine red.

ZIMOROWIC

In Motion

Look at Lvov, how its tall walls
Raise their towers from where ground crawls
Up into brightness, coloured bright.
With their tops, as is only right,
They touch the heavens. The hills which grip
The city join in a ring and skip,
Their hands still intertwining. The fields
Clap in the valleys. The dark wood yields
Its voice in song and copses join in.
To this wedding, through this sweet din,
The town sends out its citizens.
Old and young, in twos and tens,
The people follow in a herd.
Before the bride, so well prepared,
Maidens and children throw down flowers.
The maidens chant, the children throwers
Stand in a circle, bow thrice to the ground.

The Poet's Rhymes

We more than any others, shepherds, we
Should always blow the pipes and always be
Away from useless noise, in mountains or
Tenantless wilderness or forest's core.
The birds which greet each morning give us new
Beginnings to our melody, sung true.
The winds and rills which loudly tread on stones
Whisper their music to us with sweet moans.
Echo speaks with us in the lowest vales
Rhyming our word with sound that never stales.
We never couple verses : Echo's strains
To our first add a second which remains.

24

ZIMOROWIC

Epitaph

My wedding dress is just a winding sheet :
A handful of earth my dowry when I meet ,
The worm, my bridegroom : the grave, my marriage bed:
My children are the tears my parents shed.

Ignacy KRASICKI (1735–1801)

The Lamb and the Wolves

The predator's excuse is always good.
Two wolves attacked a lamb in a dark wood.
It said : "I want your legal rights defined."
"You're weak and tender ; and it's dark." They dined.

Caged Birds

The young finch asked the old one why he wept :
"There's comfort in this cage where we are kept."
"You who were born here may well think that's so
But I knew freedom once, and weep to know."

The Master and the Dog

Because of thieves, a dog barked all night through.
His master, sleepless, beat him black and blue.
On the next night the dog slept ; and thieves came.
The silent dog was beaten all the same.

The Heron, the Fish and the Crab

A heron growing old, as they often do,
A little blind and crooked also grew,
And when she couldn't catch another fish
Thought of a ruse to fill her empty dish.
She said to the fish: "You don't know
Why I am weeping so."
So they asked her to tell
And they listened well.
"Yesterday
I heard them say
The fishermen who work
Here by day and by dark
That they were weary
Their labour dreary,
'Let's empty the pond and we'll take the lot.
There's not much they can do when the pond's dry but rot.'"
The fish wept, and the heron sedate
Said: "I pity your fate.
There's but one thing for you
And that's what you must do.
Another pond's nearby
Which they will never dry.
Make it your home. Go there.
Fly through the splendid air."
"O take us," cried the fish
But the heron didn't wish
To help them, and gave way
Reluctantly to their plea.
One at a time she flew off with them in her beak
And swallowed them without a squeak.
Bloated with fish, she thought she would like some crabs.
One of them, smelling treachery, grabs
Her by the neck as she flies over the ground
And, well, she perishes without a sound.
And so all sly
Traitors die.

27

Franciszek ZABŁOCKI (1754–1821)

Denunciation

I write about our hosts of cheats and liars
Who'd sell their souls if such souls could find buyers.
Should God abet my labours, then this work
Will please the learned and instruct the Turk.
But I implore my public to abjure
All praise of me till my success is sure.
I shall expect no laurels and no fame
Till one damned rascal hangs himself for shame.

Franciszek KARPIŃSKI (1741–1825)

Recollection of Past Love
(a pastoral song)

Within the vale the stream runs on.
Sycamores shield it with their boughs.
I think of evenings long since gone
When you, Justine, and I made vows.

Night passed too quickly : then pale day
Allowed one single last caress.
Our love had stolen sleep away.
Love feeds upon our sleeplessness.

Dawn whitened earth. We saw on each
Sycamore diamond signatures.
We sat unmoving, without speech,
And carved our names, my name and yours.

No one sneered, and no one knew ;
Heaven alone watched over us.
There was no guilt between us two.
Heaven did not think me infamous.

Look answered look as hand clasped hand.
Two mouths, made one, drank from one bowl.
Our bodies learned to understand
And soul, when asked, replied to soul.

Then thunder came : a storm arose :
An ancient oak fell like a stone :
And, trembling as you held me close,
You said, "I will not die alone."

Here, to this stream, that apple tree,
I often come and try to think.
My thirst was never slaked till she
With her own hands gave me to drink.

29

But nothing in this world will keep.
Fate parts us, angry Fate, and blind.
A country yokel tending sheep
Has blotted out the names we signed.

No, there is not a single trace.
The wood is overgrown and sere.
The stream, the sycamores, keep their place,
But you, Justine, you are not here.

Letter of Excuse

You don't know how the snow and wind
Beat down and make these deaf walls blind.
I stuck my nose out, took a peep,
The snow was half way up, *so deep*.

The wild beast's run to his warm den.
Frost's crossed the river, bearing men.
The raven's the one bird I hear
—And he just loves his weather blear.

When I still rode my wooden horse,
They talked of death, the famous Tsar's :
Peter, how he was dragged to hell
When the wind blew, the frost was snell.

For there was such a snowstorm then!
Ravens flew down, then up again.
The night fell into the midst of day.
And O the yarns that float away !

Well, I won't budge today for you.
Upon my soul, I swear that's true.
I shall sit here by my warm grate,
Refusing to share Great Peter's fate.

Franciszek Dionizy KNIAŹNIN (1750–1807)

Composed during a Journey

With love's bolt buried in my heart I could
Not travel far on this unwilling trip.
I wanted to stay near my greatest good
And drink the nectar of companionship.
We, and we only, understand the mystery
    Who make its secret history.

Past joys reproached me, joys that had been short
But now prolonged my longing, night and day.
Affliction pained me though sweet birds made sport :
Swan's down seemed rough ; and blue skies looked like grey.
Nor could friends help : no witty conversation
    Changed my grief's persuasion.

Except that I am always sorrowing
I don't know what goes on within my heart.
The flame is constant and my ardours ring
True—as you know they have rung from the start.
Real love has kindled it : the bright flame dances
    Within my inmost fancies.

You yourself witnessed my acute distress
When I left Warsaw, though I loved the town.
And Minsk was worse : what sadness names compress !
Sieltse misted as my tears fell down.
Wisnitsa, where I spent the night in sorrow,
    Promised no tomorrow.

Both Brzesc and Terespol wondered to see
Such love as Love has forced me to confess.
Koden, Rozanka : boredom, misery :
Yet there I sang of loving tenderness.
In each a song was offered you, my treasure.
    And grief to give you pleasure.

But now my bitterness is almost over.
I can begin to count the minutes now.
Soon, at your feet, your ever-constant lover
Will kneel down humbly to renew his vow
Of steadfast faith, and pledge himself once more
        To suffer and adore.

To Whiskers

Oh whiskers, ornamental and so twirly,
    Unmanly youths deny your beauty,
And Polish women turn all girly-girly
    To jeer at you, forgetting their duty.

But when the sabre measures whole frontiers
    And the martial gaze plumbs all hearts
The god of love on whiskers then appears
    To aim his painless darts.

And when our knights departed at the gate
    Each visage bore a sign of its own
And every Jenny whispered to each Kate :
    "For such black whiskers I'd lie down."

When the old Czarnecki covered iron with fame
    Offering his country his life's blood
Though all Polish women worshipped him the same
    He twirled his whiskers where he stood.

When Vienna greeted John the Third a cry
    Went up from every German frau :
"The Polish king who saved us has come by,
    God bless his royal whiskers now."

But now sad changes fall out of the gloom
    And Nice abhors the knightly face.
Instead some Dorant dripping with perfume
    Sneers at whiskers and our brave race.

They're not ashamed of either parents or brothers
    So let them deride their country's soul.
As for me, I'm proud I'm not like all the others :
    I'll twirl my whiskers, being a Pole.

Julian NIEMCEWICZ (1757–1841)

Written on the Coach-box
Between Cheltenham and London, September 24th, 1832

Wherever on an English road you go
A town, each village : all the fields aglow :
A garden country : stacks of fertile corn
Hurry on carts and no lane is forlorn.
The fat herds graze upon the gay green wealds
And Freedom's hand guides ploughshares over fields.
Those ships there, rising from the ocean, bring
Riches from all the world and, emptying
Her horn, great Plenty looks and joys to see
A people strong by toil and liberty.

Antoni MALCZEWSKI (1793–1826)

Open Spaces

The warriors gone, these fields are void and still.
Even regret for heroes cannot fill
The heart's emptiness. And the eye loiters here,
Restlessly finding nothing really clear,
No movement and no calm. The sun slants down.
A black crow and its shadow sometimes clown.
They croak. A cricket chirrups from a clump
Of nearby grass. The air appears to slump.
And why does nothing from the past descend
Gently, ancestrally, now? no august blend
Of grief and exaltation burden us?
Descend indeed, by paths laborious
Beneath the earth to reach a skeleton
Dressed in the armour of some knight unknown.
There, with the rust and ashes, corpses rot,
Warm flesh where worms are hatching. Here, man's thought
Without an aim or limit, like Despair,
Strays over fields, unsheltered by the air.

After the Battle

The hill beside the wood had dressed in green
And spread thyme round it in a fragrant screen.
The wind caressed the trees as though it knew
Why the white birches bent like young girls who
Cast tearful shadows when a knight is killed.
That healing haze from which sleep is distilled
Attacked both victors and the prisoners then.
For one thing's sure : shame, glory, pleasure, pain,
Boredom and toil, exhaust us equally.
In front of them, a fire about to die
Threw its last glow across the battlefield.
Far back, above the wood, the sun had wheeled
The likeness of a camp-fire through the trees.
All else was greying. Ravenous colonies
Of carrion birds were shrieking overhead.
Sentries took guard. The camp-fire noises spread.
Men flitted to and fro ; and horses crunched
Grass till it tinkled like distant armour.

The Window Curtain

He watched the full moon topple his full height
On the black grass among the shapes of night.
Serene and bright her revolutions run!
But then her eyes are fixed upon the sun.
The knight's head bowed. Her smile derisively
Lit her plump features as she watched him sigh.
Grief filled his mind. Confused emotions wrought
A void that killed remorse and stilled all thought.
Remembrance lapsed. All joys hung in suspense,
All loves, and each accoutrement of sense.
He neared the sleeping house, silent as it.
Its muteness was by one pale treasure lit,
One rich enchantment like an Arabian tale's.
But what was that? His courage almost fails
Until he sees above his black despair
An opening bedroom window brightening where,
As though directing travellers through the trees,
A flimsy curtain flirts with the coy breeze,
Drawing the wind into the room, and then
Modestly pushing it away again.
O what a pleasant flood of fire then steals
Through every vein! What happiness he feels!
Who could resist? That madness scorched his bones.
He was no virtuous statue made of stones.
His arts were courteous faith, to love and fight.
He reached her room in seconds. But delight
Withered. The bed was neat. Maria lay
There in her funeral robes.

Adam MICKIEWICZ (1798–1855)

To Guests

If you wish to charm your host, carefully follow this advice :
On arriving, never announce what everyone knows quite well,
That at some other place they're dining, that the Countess's ball
    was sheer Hell,
That corn is cheap, water is wet, Greek robbers wear lice.

In the drawing room, observe the young couple who look so nice :
Do they nod to get out of your way ? or linger to chat for a spell ?
Do they sit apart from each other, as though each was wrapped
    in a shell ?
All in good time. They unrumple. They are really as quiet as mice.

If the lady laughs when one smiles and, laughing, still looks glum ;
If the gentleman glimpses one sideways as though suspicious of
    treason,
Examines his watch, puts it back, then dangles it on his thumb,

Regarding one's clothes politely, with hatred not meant to
    displease one,
You should know what to say : Goodbye ; it was such a pleasure
    to come.
You can visit that house again, but wait until next season.

Bajdary

I whip my horse into the wind and see
Woods, valleys, rocks, tumbling and tussling, agleam,
Flow on and disappear like the waves of a stream :
I want to be dazed by this whirlpool of scenery.

And when my foaming horse will not obey,
When the world grows colourless caught in a dark beam,
Woods, valleys and rocks pass in a bad dream
Across the broken mirror of my parched eye.

Earth sleeps, not me. I jump in the sea's womb.
The big black wave roars as it rushes ashore.
I bend my head, stretch out like a bridegroom

Toward the wave breaking. Surrounded by its roar
I wait till whirlpools drive my thoughts to doom,
A boat capsized and drowned : oblivion's core.

The Prisoner's Return

Him! So I rushed. "But there will be a spy.
Don't go today." I made another try
The morning after. Police thugs at the door.
The next week, too, I went. "His health is poor."
And then, at last, when travelling out of town
They told me that a fat but broken-down
Fellow was my friend. His hair had gone ; his skin
Was a puffed sponge that wrinkles burrowed in.
Bad food had done it, that and rotten air.
I never would have known him, sitting there.
I said good day. He couldn't place my face.
I introduced myself, but not a trace
Of recognition. Then I reminded him
Of this and that. His glance grew deep, kept dim.
And all his daily tortures, all the fears
Of sleepless nights, and all the thoughts, the years,
I saw ; but only for a moment : then
A monstrous veil descended once again.
His pupils, like thick glass refracting light,
Looked grey when stared at but could shine with bright
Patterns of rainbows when glimpsed from the side.
Cobwebs are like that too : their grey threads hide
Sparks and rust-reds and spots of black and green :
Yet in those pupils nothing could be seen.
Their surface, quite opaquely, showed that they
Had lain a long time in the damp dark clay.

Next month I called on him, hoping to find
A man at ease, refreshed, in his right mind.
But many questioners had had their say,
Ten thousand sleepless nights had passed away,
Too many torturers had probed, and he
Had learned that shadows make good company
And silence is the only right reply.

The city, in a month, could not defy
The laws that had been taught him year by year.
Day was a traitor, sunlight a spy : his fear
Made turnkeys of his family, hangmen of guests.
The door's click meant: "More questions. More arrests."
He'd turn his back, prop head on hand, and wait
Collecting strength enough to concentrate.
His lips pressed tight to make them one thin line.
He hid his eyes lest they should give some sign,
And any sign might tell them what he thought.
The simplest question seemed to have him caught.
He'd crouch in shadows, crying "I won't talk."
Because his mind was made of prison rock
So that his cell went with him everywhere.
His wife wept long, kneeling beside his chair.
But maybe it was mostly his child's tears
That, finally, released him from his fears.

I thought he'd tell his story in the end.
(Ex-convicts like to speak to an old friend
About their prison days.) I'd learn the truth,
The truth that tyrants hide, the Polish truth.
It flourishes in shadows. Its history
Lives in Siberia where its heroes die,
There and in dungeons. But what did my friend say ?
He said he had forgotten. And, with dismay,
I listened to his silence. His memory was
Written upon, and deeply, but, because
It had long rotted in the dark, my friend
Could not read what was written : "We'd better send
For God. He will remember and tell us all."

Inner Monologue

Then Wojski, finished with the chase, comes home ;
But Telimena hunts the deepest room
Of the deserted manor. She doesn't move :
Arms crossed, she sits, and sees her swift thoughts rove
In search of two bright beasts she plans to run
To earth together and capture either one.
The Count—Tadeusz. The Count, she argues thus,
A likely heir and deftly courteous,
And he's in love—a little—and today.
He's not the marrying kind. And anyway
She is the elder and his relatives might
Object. She's poor. The world won't think it right.

Then Telimena stood upon her toes.
Her diligent eye, still proud but now morose
Studied the mirror where she saw her breast,
As she leant sideways, wander half-undressed.
She asked her body for advice. She sighed
Then sat, eyes lowered, while her mind replied.

The Count's a lord—no faithful servant—and
He's blond, his nature cool, his passions bland.
Tadeusz is just a lad, a pleasant boy,
A child whose first love fills him with child joy.
He's in her debt and if she's careful he
Will be as true to her as youth can be
—And earnest youngsters, though their thoughts may rove,
Have hearts more steadfast than a grandsire's love.
A young man's virgin heart gives everything
That gratitude for love's first joys can bring.
Gayly he shares the sweets of love with one
Good friend, and gayly leaves her when they're done.
Only the old drunk with his guts burnt up
Curses what drowns him as he tilts the cup.

To Telimena all these things made sense
Since she had brains and much experience.
But then, what could *they* say? But who were *they*?
She'd find a love-nest well out of their way
Or—even better—quit them one and all
And take up residence in the capital.
There she'd display her young man to the *monde*
And guide his steps and teach him to be fond,
Advise him like a brother—that was it;
And take what joys her years would still permit.

She paced her alcove, gay and determined now,
With lowered head and gay determined brow.

Over the great clear pool

Over the great clear pool
Rocks ranged in steep files :
Water, transparent and cool,
Reflected their black faces.

Over the great clear pool
Black clouds chased for miles :
Water, transparent and cool,
Reflected their dwindling traces.

Over the great clear pool
Lightning burst, thunder spread.
Water, transparent and cool,
Reflected the light : the sound fled.
Clear as before, the pool
Lay, transparent and cool.

This pool surrounds me and
I reflect what's to see
Whether the rocks still stand
Or lightning flashes free.

Black rocks forebode me ill.
The clouds have rain to spill.
Loud lightning has to glow.
I have to flow, to flow . . .

Juliusz SŁOWACKI (1809–1849)

Hymn

Master, my heart is sore. Your radiant West
Pours out its rainbows for me, while your deep
Blue waters quench the star that burns in quest
    Of everlasting sleep :
Yet though you gild the skyline, sea and shore,
    Master, my heart is sore.

Erect, like empty husks of corn, I am
Void of both pleasure and satiety.
Greeting a stranger, I can still seem calm
    Though silent as this sky.
In front of you I must say something more.
    Master, my heart is sore.

Petulant as an infant when his mother
Leaves him alone, I see the sky grow red.
Its last beams rise from water as I smother
    The tear I almost shed.
Though dawn will bring fresh daylight as before,
    Master, my heart is sore.

Today I watched, wedged in the blue air,
A convoy of storks, and they were flying
A hundred miles from land, still more to where
    This long low land is lying.
I've seen storks race across my native moor.
    Master, my heart is sore.

Since I have meditated much on death,
Since I have seldom known a home, since I
Am a poor pilgrim, trudging, out of breath,
    And lightning scars the sky :
Since time still keeps my unknown grave in store,
    Master, my heart is sore.

Perhaps my skeleton will whiten and
No gravestone cast its solemn shadow there,
I shall still grudge each corpse the plot of land
    That keeps it safe from air.
My bed will be as restless as it's poor.
    Master, my heart is sore.

At home a child will pray for me each day
Just as he has been told. And yet I know
That, as it sails, this ship takes me away,
    A mile each mile we go.
And since his prayers cannot the child restore,
    Master, my heart is sore.

A hundred years from now some other men
Will watch the rainbows that your angels hew
Across the starry vastness—but by then
    They will be dying too.
I reach out toward the nothing at my core.
    Master, my heat is sore.
                Composed at sea off Alexandria.

A Carol

Now Jesus visits earth.
The whole world finds rebirth
Et mentes.

File past the manger's stall
Small angels and more small
Ridentes.

Sparrows chase each other
Round the Virgin mother
Cantantes.

Swan stitch the simple air :
Their down shines silver there
Mutantes.

With down she makes a pillow
And puts it in a hollow
For the Child.

With hay she makes his cot
Warm as the smallest thought
That ever smiled.

Give me a mile of land

Give me a mile of land—or even less.
A piece of turf would serve me, friends, if there
You placed a man, one man whose fearlessness
Had freed him, soul and body, from despair.
Within his brain I'd work my spells to show
A statue with two faces, both aglow.

Give me a planet smaller than the moon,
A golden squadron tinkling from its tail,
And let it skim the forests, let its croon
Be hallowed by one patriot's dying wail :
Then shall I fetch unknown angelic things
And stand, wings open, on that star that sings.

When I, my friends, implore my God to grant
Me a poor country and the right to fight,
I seem to see our chivalries aslant
The thunder of our enemies in flight.
Hot in pursuit, I reach the stars : then sleek
Sneers of sharp light ask crudely what I seek.

Stars, you are cold small Satans made of clay,
Intense with disbelief. And I, half-crazed,
Am broken by your hate. Dreams make me say
That Poland burns already : and I have raised
Fountains of flame to prove my country could.
But all that burns is my own heart—like wood.

Farewell

When any poet's brightest glory shines
His words construct a statue from his fears :
Centuries will not wipe away these lines
Nor dry their tears.

While you go off into a distant land
I'm left alone to watch my exile dribble
Slowly away toward death ; or, pen in hand,
To sit and scribble.

That Angel burning at my left side

That Angel burning at my left side
Harps on an old string. And I am with you
Among the plains where white seagulls ride,
Locked in a coffin in the Siberian snow.
Hyenas howl out of the wind. Reindeer
Graze on the graves, under your sure care.

The roots of lilies probe my corpse. It shines,
A white goblet wonderfully transformed,
A lantern corpse that fills the night with signs,
—And the music of the soul makes silence alarmed.
You dim the lamp and ask the music to
Keep silent that my spirit may sleep through.

Alone, you say your prayers. You go on speaking
Into the holy sapphire. And from your hair,
Like diamonds, a chain of stars is streaking
Into the heavens—and each star is a prayer.

Zygmunt KRASIŃSKI (1812–1859)

God has denied me the angelic measure

God has denied me the angelic measure
That marks a poet in the world of thought.
Had I possessed it earth would become a treasure
But I'm a rhymer since I have it not.

Oh, my heart rings with heavenly zones of sound
But ere they reach my lips they break apart.
Men hear a clattering when I'm around
But day and night I hear my aching heart.

It beats against my waves of blood : a star
Rings in the vast blue whirlpool of the sky.
Men in their festive halls don't hear so far :
God listens to the star until it dies.

Cyprian NORWID (1821–1883)

Conversation Piece

And they talked about Chopin again,
—Our *foremost* artist, you know :
"I like his Polish *dash*, that racy glow ;
He's no sad mumbler in the romantic vein.
And though I can't say what I mean by art
I do know music : it unlocks my heart
And captures me and makes itself at home :
I doubt if most musicians know as much
About the sounds they make or the strings they touch."

Bogumil said : "That's quite a mouthful ; but, accepting the lot
I would still rather examine an artist's *thought*.
I'd prefer to ask whether he spoke the whole truth of his nation,
Whether he was able to make a complete confession within his
       form of creation,
Or whether he was ashamed of the truth's vulgarity
So that he had to stifle it to get quick popularity,
Whether he buried truth or the truth buried him :
That's the test, and it doesn't depend on my personal whim."

"Now, now. Why moralise ?—and at such length too,"
Konstanty broke in from among the young men.
"Since they're all make-believe, what has truth got to do
With the imitations of nature that artists conceive ?
Music would mean nothing if
I had to parse it like a hieroglyph.
Bogumil's notions would force us all to receive
Absolution from a mazurka.
What's beautiful is for us all
And doesn't need a *confessional*.
Rain, rain, go to Spain :
Old Bogumil's at his tricks again."
Then many people applauded with laughter
To show that good sense had been charmingly said.

52

They had no conversation about art thereafter
Since the truth had been demonstrated and they were well-bred.
But the musicians around the rostrum
Discussed composition in terms of the part
It plays in transforming life into the life of art.

Those who love

A woman, parents, brothers, even God
Can still be loved, but those who love them need
Some physical vestige, shadow : I have none.
Cracow is silent now that its hewn stone
Has lost what tongue it had ; no banner of
Mazovian linen has been stained to prove
Art obstinate ; the peasant's houses tilt ;
The native ogives of our churches wilt ;
Barns are too long ; our patron saints are bored
With being statues ; partitioned and ignored,
Form, from the fields to steeples, can't command
One homespun wand or touch one angel's hand.

But just to see

But just to see a chapel like this room,
No bigger : there to watch Polish symbols loom
In warm expanding series which reveal
Once and for all the Poland that is real.
There the stone-cutter, mason, carpenter,
Poet, and, finally, the knight and martyr
Could re-create with pleasure, work and prayer.
There iron, bronze, red marble, copper could
Unite with native larches, stone with wood,
Because those symbols, burrowed by deep stains,
Run through us all as ores run through rock veins.

Fate

Mischance, ferocious, shaggy, fixed its look
On man, gazed at him, deathly grey,
And waited for the time it knew he took
To turn away.

But man, who is an artist measuring
The angle of his model's elbow joint,
Returned that look and made the churlish thing
Serve his aesthetic point.
Mischance, the brawny, when the dust had cleared
Had disappeared.

The Metropolis

This street—a street
In any city : over them all the *cross*.
Window-panes, juggling sunlight, sometimes cheat :
Twinkling like cat's eyes but no mouse to toss.

Pedestrians, in mournful black, go by :
The stoic's colour, but
They shout, rush, crush, stifle each other, cry,
Each in his jostled rut.

Two forces only, and two gestures here :
Factory owners search despair—*(for fun?)*—
Then those who work, and fifty times a year
Gloat over what they've won.

Two tremors and two images, just two :
Buy property in heaven before you're dead
Or manufacture *ecstasy* with a few
Crusts of stale bread.

An Arab, in his priestly clothes, goes by,
A ray of stillness in the rush of clouds.
He is carved ivory.
My eye can rest. Let its repose be proud.

And then a funeral. At last no rush.
The side-street crowd respects death's dignity.
I follow it. My fretful gestures hush.
Here let me rest my eye.

O fellow creatures with no fellows, I
Plunge through my thoughts above you—no great loss.
A small balloon glints in the blue sky.
And through the clouds ? Yes. Yes. It *is* the cross.

Recipe for a Warsaw novel

Three landlords, stupid ones ; cut each in two ;
    That'll make six : add stewards, Jews and water
Enough to give full measure : whip the brew
    With one pen, flagellate your puny jotter :
Warm, if there's time, with kisses : that's the cue
    For putting in your blushing gushing daughter
Red as a radish : tighten up : add cash,
A sack of roubles, cold : mix well, and mash.

Sequence from a Poem

Berries. Wild berries. Their linen flowers
Fell and went puff-puff, playing with the wind
In the soft distance, while the fruit
Blushed. A carpet gleamed from green.
Our horses trod it gently.
We didn't ask the road : we knew roads
And paths and slopes, and the flat stones
Thrown down for a bridge, water above them waving
A polished window pane . . .
                     we traipsed about
Purposely, faultlessly, Rosy and I,
Two other guests, only two, in attendance,
Casually, pleasantly—(we were all strangers)—
And Uncle Solomon would wait on us most ably
Either with luncheon
Or those juicy suppers we took in the garden
While a white moth looked everywhere for light, or a glow-
Worm flew through deep shadows in the alley
Alive with a spark . . .
                the very air was blessed
In the lungs as they breathed, in the heart as it beat, in the spirit :
In order to feel that air you must know a Polish village,
A world half idyll
And half a caprice of the *monde*,
Above history or, maybe, *beyond* it—
I couldn't say. It's a separate world,
Similar, perhaps to those Happy Isles of the ancients,
Full of the charm of history, but free from its strain, its continual
    effort.

It is there that the spirits so blissfully blessed
Allow a little politics, enough to season
Their weighty observations
In the alley which looks so serious under its immortal trees.

With a solemn kind of zest they deliver pronouncements,
With some sort of sacred pathos, a
Brutus-like shadow, the shadow of Cato utters words,
Words about Philippi . . .
It would seem that politics and history,
Urging to temporal tasks and duties, don't matter much ;
For temporal history doesn't
Turn to them. It doesn't turn to everyone, it would seem.
Only a Jew occasionally by the road,
Like an old obelisk, a remnant from the Pharaohs,
Reminds us of the ages. Then, too, it sometimes happens that
A peasant, cracking his plough against it,
Uncovers a piece of armour and throws it on a dyke : the small
    boys play
Music on it : or, maybe, it will happen that
In some castle hall or other
(Where fruit lies drying) a blackened portrait
Slips down, dragging its rusty nail.
So much for history. As a phenomenon
It remembers its dignity here
In a series of near
Accidents.

Władysław SYROKOMLA (1823–1862)

The Raven
(A Lithuanian Song)

From above the wood, from over the cloud
    On to the village square
A black-winged raven fell like a shroud
    And called its young to good fare.
Oh, it had eaten on a bleak
    Grave in a battlefield.
It held a blood-smeared hand in its beak,
    A ring with the blood congealed.

"Oh, raven, raven, how have you come ?
    Has the storm blown you right ?
This golden ring in your beak is dumb
    And this hand so white ?"
"Beyond the mountain, maiden fair,
    A mighty battle I found ;
Rivers of young blood flowed there
    And heads fell all around.

Now the peasants are burying those
    Heroic heads I saw,
Throwing sharp gravel down to close
    Eyes like an eagle's claw.
On mounds, like grave-diggers, howl the wolves.
    Many a mother weeps
Over a grave as the day revolves
    Into a night that sleeps."

A groan tore at the maiden's breast,
    She buried her face in her hand :
"Oh, misery, how I was blest,
    This sorrow I can't stand.
I know who died in suffering,
    To whom this hand belongs.
I gave my lover this golden ring
    In return for his songs."

SYROKOMLA

From the Madhouse

Lord of this world, I rise,
Which walks, swims, creeps and flies.
Heaven and earth are all mine
And so they will remain.
I've locked up heaven, you see,
And pocketed the key.
No hand will snatch my strings
That tie up earthly things.
Sit in your mud, sit quiet.
Breathe not a word, no riot.
Or I'll pull faces and swear
Till you break up from fear.
Silence. I'm wearying.
Dim that sun—my eyes sting.
If still too bright in space
Shave skull away from rays
As they have shaved my head
For the pink light it shed.

Epitaph for a country Squire: *D.O.M.*

He beat his peasants till
They bought gin from his still.
He owned a hundred cottages
And ate his borsch with sausages.
Sipping beer, he collected
Rents, and was much respected.
Sometimes, he'd play at cards
On feasts, in the inn yards,
And talk to mine Jewish host
Over a mutton roast
About the possibility
Of peace or war and why.
One day at breakfast he ate
A leg of lamb, and ate
A hundred meat balls, tasty
With lashings and lashings of pastry.
His tummy-aches, you see,
Took him to eternity.
And now he rests at last.
In the grave he sleeps fast,
Dozing while ages travel
Overhead on the gravel.
He'll wake when an angel cries:
"Master, it's time to rise.
Steady, there now, steady.
Your roast beef is ready."

Adam ASNYK (1838–1897)

Grey·Horse

Grey horse, you don't know : grey horse, you don't know.
    Why are you musing so ?
You don't know the road, don't know the road
    To my darling across the snow.

My love has forsaken you and me.
    Without a word she has gone.
Unless you find the road to her
    We must both search on and on.

Grey horse, we'll outrun : grey horse, we'll outrun.
    It will be hard to keep pace.
We'll outrun this wind which is blowing
    We shall not rest from our chase.

Grey horse, my heart : grey horse, my heart :
    My heart weighs more than I :
For it has lost all thought of hope
    And it doesn't even know why.

Maria KONOPNICKA (1842–1910)

A Vision

Spring comes : the flowers learn their coloured shapes.
I look at them, but back at me there gapes
　　　　Emptiness, white and endless.

And Summer comes to where the gold crops stand ;
But I still see, as plain as my own hand,
　　　　Emptiness white and endless.

And death will come to dim my human sight.
My eyes, inside the tomb, will watch with fright
　　　　Emptiness, white and endless.

At midnight, from my coffin, I shall go
Thoughtfully toward the distant fields that show
　　　　Emptiness, white and endless.

Stanisław WYSPIAŃSKI (1869–1907)

The Poet and the Peasant Bride

Bride: In a carriage of huge gold
I met the devil, my dream.
Such nonsense I'm always told
belongs to the world of *seem.*

Poet: But the devil dropped from some place
and, of course, the carriage of gold.

Bride: In a dream it's not surprising.
Don't mock me, sir, I'll be bold.
Anything can appear in dreams.
You yourself make up things by day
and write them down in reams
as though you had something—when there's nothing
—to say.

Poet: Some people pay. And out of the marriage
Of two dreams like that
you can get a proper carriage
and a devil dressed in a hat:
the crowds will lap it up.

Bride: I was so tired of the dance.
I dreamt I stood on the carriage step
my eyes drooping—oh, the romance!
I dreamt I sat in the carriage
and, as we moved through the woods, I asked
"Where are you taking me, devils?"
"To Poland," they said, although masked.
And where is that Poland, where is it?
I ask you, sir, do you know?

Poet: You could pay the whole world a visit
and watch it grow and grow
but Poland you'd never find.

Bride: It can't be very big.

Poet: Put, Jagusia, your hand
      —for there is a cage, a twig
      under your breast.

Bride: Right.
      It's the dart in my bodice
      sewn up a bit too tight.

Poet: And what do you feel beat?

Bride: This isn't much of a lesson:
      my heart in all this heat.

Poet: And that is your Poland.

Let nobody weep over my grave

Let nobody weep over my grave
except my wife.
Your dogged tears I easily waive
and your feigned grief.

Let neither a bell croak over my pall
nor someone sing with a shriek;
but the rain may sob at my funeral
and the wind creak.

Whoever wants to, may throw handfuls of earth
until I'm choked by the mound.
The sun will shine at its fine new birth
and burn away my wound.

And then, perhaps, once more, maybe,
bored with lying down,
I'll break that house enclosing me
and run to the sun.

And when you see me in my flight
a bright figure up there,
call me back if you like my light
in the language I knew down here.

Maybe I'll hear it there above,
passing a star's brow;
and maybe I'll take on again, for love,
this task which is killing me now.

WYSPIAŃSKI

How can I calm myself

How can I calm myself—
full of fear are these eyes of mine,
full of terror these thoughts of mine,
full of shudders these lungs of mine,
full of panic this heart of mine—
How can I calm myself?

Lucjan RYDEL (1870–1918)

The Rainbow

Beyond Cracow there stands a black wood
And on this wood a rainbow stood.
    She is further away than ever
    Beyond the seventh river,
God binds us by the rainbow on that wood.

God made a bridge across the heavens
Out of stripes coloured in sevens.
    Oh, angels, bear the weight
    Of my heart to her feet
Across that rainbow which spans heavens.

Kazimierz TETMAJER (1865–1940)

In the Sistine Chapel

The wounded bison roars from all these walls.
That Christ—angelic cyclops—thunder falls.
A skull in agony, accursed despair,
Fury and groans : even the whimpers blare.
His brush on paint sparked like an axe on stone
And mountains powdered and their ruins moan.
Deaf though they are, these eyes, unflinching, scan
This work of a volcano, not of man.

Tadeusz MICIŃSKI (1873–1919)

Good-bye

Good-bye (how strange is the bell's tolling)
Good-bye (love is much like dying)
Good-bye (leaves from the tree are falling)
Good-bye (what is the wind crying ?)
  Never again!
     Your heart is weeping.
  Suddenly it burst, sliced—
  Fare well—it must be—and you, in God's keeping—
  Pity!
    To horse ! Oh, my Lord Christ—

Jan KASPROWICZ (1860–1926)

The Sunset

Blessed be this moment
When the evening hymn of the soul seeks music,
the spotless, humble and meek soul—
He was and we were before the beginning.
Let us praise and worship his holy name.

Light of sunset, why don't you fade
into the ocean of these thick vapours
which have buried my sun?
The moon hoists itself up over the coiling mountains,
touches the edges of clouds with silver
and illuminates the crevices of snow.
Night steals quietly down from the east:
its great calm rests on the slopes—
And yet you glow.
An echo crawls towards the soul
from those far distant plains
that fall asleep beyond a hundred waters
across a thousand roads.
Silence.
This is the croon of the boy's old tune:
Oh, my fife, play for me, play.
I've made you out of the twig of a willow,
there where the blue stream silvers a hollow,
and there where the wood sprites follow—
oh!
At dawn I ploughed my plot
from field to field, the lot,
but cockle grew to blot
all my corn out.
Oh, my fife, play for me, play,
play for me. . . .
And why do you still glow?
Once and for all, let it be put out.

The mountain ash blushes,
the old linden gushes,
dust from the road rises in bushes—
Oh, light of sunset, why can't you keep quiet?
Why—with this fiery cry
shooting from that precipice
between these two hell walls—
do you blind me so and deafen
that I cannot reach my end?
My day has already died
but its sunset light still bleeds
as if it were to bleed into eternity.
It eats all things with its flames,
burning my world and burning my soul.
From the gigantic sheaves of fire
thrashed by invisible flails
the seeds of sparks fall round
into the sky, on to the earth.
The moon has caught fire:
in a moment it has grown
into a huge flaming sphere;
it breaks into pieces
and tumbles in fiery lumps
on to the scorched bodies of mountains,
on to the ashes of the burnt spruce.
The lakes are in flames,
the hundred waters burn
and the thousand roads!
From the crazy entrails of the earth
volcanoes explode,
and the stars lash with lightning
the foaming floods of flames—
and with a crash
in the red ravage, perish.
God,
why do you punish me?
You stand in the glowing space,
yourself aflame, bigger than the space,
an enormous fiery cross in your hand,
and you hurl the world at me as it burns.

73

Landscape on the Move

Me.
It's me. I'm weeping,
flapping my own wings.
I am the bird in the morning
and the late night-bird.
My eyes are bloodshot, yet I've got to look
right into the sun.
At my feet
they are digging a lonely grave.
A crow—that's black—
sits on an outstretched cross
and it croaks
and it croaks and pecks
dead bits of dust with its restless beak.

They stagger on:
August shimmers round them with its mists;
uneasily, like shadows,
they stagger forward toward the big grave.
And behind them, the mulleins,
a procession that starts at the dunes,
and the yarrows set out from the balks
and the wild lilac sets out from beyond the fences:
sweet flag rustles in a few holes;
its roots smell sweet as it shakes off slime,
but it follows too.
And the moor contributes bulrush and thistles,
yellow spears of the thistle
lining long roads,
and the wide-leaved burdock,
the coltsfoot that's sleepy,
the violet henbane,
the thorny haw,
—they all rise
walking.

The soft leaves of the willow move
one massive formation :
they are joining the other mourners
and this is the path of mourning.

Whole fields, tricky with stubble,
have already taken off :
they have left their most native marches,
huge walls, floating in arches,
floating out over across
this great moment of loss.
And you, the Immortal,
yes, you—God,
defended by innumerable lights,
inaccessibly enthroned,
you sit tight among stiff stars,
you rest your head upon the gold Triangle ;
two trees, transformed to a cross, act for a foot-stool.
Carefully, through an hourglass, you pour the debris of
          stars.
You never even glance at the fields where we are.

Have mercy, have mercy upon us.

The Ballad of the Sunflower

My friends were flowers, but only one
   —An old blind sunflower—
Stood straight among my garden weeds
   In flowering isolation.
Night after night, I heard the wind
   Whip him with all its power.
I didn't help him much, unless
   My grief was consolation.
              What matters is dancing.

One evening I got very drunk
   —Wine's a good cure, you know.
I punched a window out and gazed
   At mountains far away.
There, they said, the snows are lying
   And stars that glitter like snow.
Damp darkness fell on my eyelids
   And all I saw looked grey.
              What matters is dancing.

Dried meadows could be seen, they said,
   And tufts of withered sedge.
Alders and leafless ash, they said,
   In bogs or by the road.
Human despairs, they said, stepped out
   Of mists at the mountains' edge
Hurrying on to the funeral
   Of the mercy of God.
              What matters is dancing.

It seems that I had brothers too
            —Death told it all to me—
How they had gone to some cruel war
            —Her kisses fleshed the tale.
And let this dark roar deeply on,
            These tears swell like the sea,
This earth they fatten with their blood
            Pant in an autumn gale.
                        What matters is dancing.

And then the sunflower, blind and old,
            Squeezed through the broken glass
Till he was in my small gay room
            Among the smells of wine.
His golden crown had long since gone.
            He'd reached a pretty pass.
His bald black head upon my breast
            Expressed his sad design.
                        What matters is dancing.

He fawned upon me like a dog
            Nuzzling against my face.
A single clumsy drop of dew
            Fell on my flushed skin,
Fell from the socket where his eye
            Had left no other trace.
The old blind sunflower kept the silence
            He shouted sorrow in.
                        What matters is dancing.

Don't mock yourself, my friend, and me :
            It's what we always get.
We're born to bless the death we die.
            My friend, can you still hear ?
The knight finds death on a high tight noose,
            Let the sturgeon choke in a net,
God himself can fall from his throne,
            Wrench and revolve the spear.
                        What matters is dancing.

My sorrow gives you no relief.
  It is a gay old sot.
Since you who once could face the sky
  Are wretched in decline
I've got a better cure than that,
  The cure that makes bones rot.
As for the soul, death's messengers,
  We'll drink it, drunken swine.
      What matters is dancing.

I tore away his last leaf then
  And picked the last seeds out :
A firm grip on his hard wood stalk
  Freed him from the ground.
Dark earth gushed in beneath the sill
  From where roots used to sprout.
The old blind sunflower must have wept
  But I heard not a sound.
      What matters is dancing.

I rose next morning—a murderer ?
  Redeemer ? who can say ?
I woke again in my small gay room
  Among the smells of wine.
The old blind sunflower, his gold crown gone,
  No longer now bore sway :
The wind no longer made him bend
  His sorrow down to mine.
      What matters is dancing.

The Day Before Harvest

One day at harvest time the sun
  Was burning up the sky;
Great Mr. Godlord took a walk
  Through oats that grew hip high.

He walked bareheaded and unbuttoned
  Examining every ear,
Wondering just what kind of crop
  He could expect this year.

And had the ploughing been quite right?
  Had the sowing been well done?
Was he, great Mr. Godlord worth
  The praise he always won?

Then in his wide left palm he crushed
  An ear or two at most,
Studied them closely, gently blew
  So that no grain was lost.

Davidson came to that same field.
  "I'll not have these oats spoiled.
This harvest is my blood and sweat.
  My wife scrimped while I toiled."

"Yours is it? That's a fine one. Mine!"
  Old Mr. Godlord spat.
"I ploughed the land, I sowed the seed.
  Poor man, you must know that.

But if you still insist, my man,
  I'll tell you what we'll do.
We'll wrestle to find out if it
  Belongs to me or you."

They grasped each other then and fought.
    Davidson's skin was torn.
God used his strength. Davidson fell
    Stone dead among the corn.

Such is the usual lot of man.
    Such things are often seen,
Men falling as fat cattle fall
    When clover's thick and green.

Old Mr. Godlord wins and smiles.
    "Brother, you must have known
These crops were mine and always will
    Be mine and mine alone."

Then in his wide left palm he crushes
    An ear or two at most,
Studies them closely, gently blows
    So that no grain is lost.

Edward SŁOŃSKI (1874–1926)

She who has not died

1

My brother, we are divided
by ill-fate and a guard :
behind two hostile ramparts
our death is our reward.

In groaning trenches we listen
to the thunder of guns :
I, your enemy, you, my enemy,
we face each other once.

The forest weeps, the earth weeps,
the whole world trembles on high.
Behind two hostile ramparts
we stand, you and I.

2

As soon as the guns begin
to roar in the dawn,
through the whistling bullets of death
your sign has always shone.

You throw at our low ramparts
your whole artillery
and you call and you speak to me :
"Brother, it is I."

The forest weeps, the earth weeps,
the whole world trembles on high,
and all the time you say to me :
"Brother, it is I."

Don't think of me, my brother,
as I march to my death :
in the fire of my bullets stand bravely
and take a deep breath.

And when you see me from afar
fire at me instead :
into a Polish heart
aim Russian lead.

For I dream of her by day
and I see her in my dreams :
She who has not died
will rise where our blood streams.

September, 1914.

Bolesław LEŚMIAN (1879–1937)

In the Dark

The lip is the lip's friend, the hand the hand's :
Lying next each other each one understands
To whom he belongs—each one of the buried dead.
Unwillingly the night goes overhead ;
The earth asserts itself, but hesitantly ;
And leaflessly the leaves move on a tree.
God stirs the wind and space : but He is high
Above the forest's distant forest sigh.
The wind says this to space : "I'll not be back
Across this forest while the night shines black."
Still darkness thickens, pierced by small starlight.
The seagulls flying over the sea are white.
One says : "I've heard the fate of stars foretold."
The next : "I've watched the heavens themselves
     unfold."
The third is silent, but because it knew
Two bodies, glowing in the darkness, who
Wove darkness into their embrace : it found
Them made of the caress in which they wound.

Brother

You would not take my hand. The dawn glow
    Made the world alter.
At that moment your brother called to you.
    For a second you faltered.

You ran to him and came back. He was dead.
    Fate, for the clouds, shone golden.
"Now I belong only to you," you said.
    Your voice broke and rolled on.

Without a glance at you, I asked : "Did he know ?"
    "Yes," you replied.
Outside, giving thoughts distance, aslant, aflow,
    The bird, as always, glided.

The Cemetery

He reached the graveyard,—grass, death, oblivion,—
He who had noticed how the world goes on.
It must have been a graveyard for dead ships.
He heard shrouds snarl under the wind's whips :
Yet quietness unravelled from the grass.
He let his silence into that silence pass.
And shaped from air a cross among the birds
While the first tombstone let him read these words :

"I did not die by chance but through the will
Of winds that found in me an easy kill.
They promised me safe anchor in my death,
Death in that anchorage : now they break faith.
The winds persist, and shipwreck underground.
New fears, not those I lost with life, resound.
Though slack with nothingness my buried forms
Are still judged worth their steerage through those storms.
Who blows the wind that makes my mainsails pout ?
Why is a ship, once started, always out ?
I can say only that, without life, this hull
Plods sleeplessly, and misery bakes the skull.
For more than plain endurance none can pray,
But pray for me to Mary, traveller, pray."

He plucked some leaves and gave them to the air,
Then knelt, and three times prayed that formal prayer.

LEŚMIAN

Memories

Those paths I brushed
With the feet of a child—where have they gone ?
    They roll down as tears do, hushed,
    Out of the eyes, down, down.

The freshness of morning would wake me up.
The sun would be painting a masterpiece.
    A golden coast—a golden pup,
    A golden guitar—a golden precipice.

Stare. Stare sufficiently into the light
From the midst of a great silence, and in a while
You are bound to see a camel shining bright,
A bright-eyed robber with a glistening smile.

At breakfast the table became a desert. I stared
Till I rode the camel and I saw the gleaming thief.
Father, assured of his safety, never despaired
But read his paper calmly, rustling a leaf.

A triple rainbow embroidered the carafe,
The tablecloth, the cupboard, father's moustache.
A wasp, entangled in the lace curtains, would laugh
And the curtains laughed too, their threads in the sun, a bright
    patch.

And the rich floor, dreamily glittering, mirrored it all :
The leaves of the palm shone brighter at the back
But melted shallowly, and a thin glaze would fall
As if someone had spilled greenery by mistake.

    The arm-chair sipping its own velvet peace
    Would grow heavier, comfortably, I think.
    The sugar would plot for a blue spark's release
    And the loaf of bread would turn pink.

The clock shakes free of its long compressed coils and booms
    A prolonged note through the hall to the sky.
In that furnished day-dreaming among the sunny rooms
    Everybody endures and does not die.

But something happened : something went wrong.
The same clock struck, but shyly, in another town.
        The soul stumbled over the body that had grown too
        strong,
        And they began to die, one by one.

87

Leopold STAFF (1878–1957)

The Fountain

The fountain is a water lily
Blossoming but too silly
To let pale fragrance pour
From its transparent flower.

The fountain is a glass wing
Fastened to a stone ring
And though wind makes it try
It won't catch a butterfly.

The fountain, the lily, the wing:
A ruse or not? What is this thing?
A spray of water, rainbow-high,
Single in its trinity.

Emil ZEGADŁOWICZ (1888–1941)

The Vagabond Crosses

The alders saddened. The cemetery
lifted its crosses higher
and played on the iron-spiked gate
as if it were a lyre—
two spiders wove a net from the wall
to where the sun was setting—
the black crosses halted in
a broken-up grating—
and they walked and walked, walked on and on,
their wood, the knocking of
their stone, the crooked shapes of them,
their Warsaw and Cracow,
their Czestochowa and Kalwaria,
across the rivers and seas,
their Lublin and Alwernia, the shades
of these ones blackened these,
knock, knock, beat on, beat they walked,
banging the shutters tight,
their echo outward focussed was
lament, departing, night;
and then at dawn they hurried on
knocking, rattling, late,
as arm in arm they made their way
towards the boreal gate,
and towards the setting sun they ran
on—on to the white North Pole,
the promised graveyard where they could
rest without a soul—
they walked and walked, walked on and on,
running, dispersing, so
they cut through drifts, deep shifting drifts
of the immemorial snow.

Tytus CZYŻEWSKI (1885–1945)

Spring, 1917
(In memoriam : Apollinaire.)

It was the earth I called to, one, two, three.
The sun is just a hole bleeding in the sky.
The dagger that dug it has long been extracted.
A scarlet clown, good Caesar Borgia,
And Richard III, hunched shadow on the wall.
Observe the moon, a sliver that sticks out
   from the sack on his shoulders.
And swallows swell within the dome of the sky,
and blossoms thicken in the fields,
and clouds divide to take up battle order :
I see Alexander the Great
   as he stands at Pompeii, in ornate mosaic ;
the banners make merry as armies emerge
   from the trenches of Verdun.
Only among the spring clouds, only there in sharp silhouette
I glimpse a green artillery helmet.
It's Lieutenant Wilhelm Kostrowicki.
An armoured engine stamps on the sky.
The thunder of spring is shaking the earth,
is probing into the guts of the earth,
is touching the human heart.
A storm will bend the biggest of trees
and leave it leafless in a wilderness of fields.
The wild vine climbs and drapes lush green
around the blackened trunk.

Julian TUWIM (1894–1953)

Wife

My husband is idle, is dumb and spends money.
He either stands still at the window or runs about town like a
bunny.

He stares and he stares, at a tram, at the sky.
He mutters, he whistles : he rummages over the house like an
amateur spy.

And then he reads books : he turns their pages at least.
There are books in the kitchen and cellar ; folios mixed with the
yeast.

But what is he thinking about ? what does my husband mumble ?
When he tries to speak he gets nervous : piles of words flurry and
tumble.

In the evening he drinks, and I feel angry enough
When I see his dear eyes getting misted up with that stuff.

His eyes are misted. He takes one more dram.
He kneels down beside me and lays his head on my arm.
It is only then that I learn for the first time who I am.

Maria PAWLIKOWSKA (1895–1945)

October

Fountains of gold! The leaves fall like gold spray.
I feel the chill in every word you wrote.
Even the sun has cooled and gone away,
Gone like a friend, and with a dying fall. A false note.

Jan LECHOŃ (1899–1956)

On the death of Joseph Conrad

Your father, too, was buried with some style.
Greek buskins seemed to clatter in the gloom
As his cortège, stiff-booted, mile by mile
Escorted him to freedom and the tomb.

Their rough tongues praised his high nobility.
Their tears were salt and wet. Like epaulettes
They placed their country on him solemnly.
Then they dispersed, in battle their regrets.

And now it's you the same wind has sucked down.
Your father in his sleepless exile calls
You in your country's language and your own
From where one lighthouse beam on all seas falls.

Stanisław MŁODOŻENIEC (1895–1959)

Moscow

```
      re        re
The  now, whe   now ?
   re    re      re
the – the   – The
            RE
        WHE   ?
        re     re        RE     re                        RE
am I the   – the    –, THE    – the   I'm – I'm – 'm THE
             RE        RE
        I'm WHE    WHE    I am
              re       re    re    re          re
Am I really the  ? – the  ? the  – the  ? really the  ?
              RE        RE
        Am I THE   ? WHE   ?

                                            re
Whether I am just there ? If there then whe   to ?
        RE        RE
        WHE   ? WHE   ?
     re       re
so the   and whe  , so

                            re          re
oh, well ! he – e – y – y – y the   too and whe   to
                    re       re
        so I'm the  , and whe   I'm
        RE
        WHE   ?
```

94

Józef CZECHOWICZ (1903–1939)

Brain 12 Years Old

Clouds lower : they are clefs,
they wade loose in the blue,
and my shoes wade in the stream
of the summer wind anew.

The shrines of St. John
enwreathed in withered mugwort,
a cloud of butterflies
has reached them—I don't know how.

Beyond that, along the road to the meadow,
on these clay hills,—
go, railway track, go.
Ivy—like ticker tape—has grown across the rails.

A path bends toward the meadow
down over the pass.
A boy foams nakedly, treading
the river grass.

There where the pines end
in front of the town,
a hundred supple branches of hands
by his brain of twelve years are thrown.

Among the corn-flower drops
on the fish-scales of water,
the brisk whim flaps
and the spiral torso.

A cry. Oh, stream ! Oh, sun !
mouth, hands stacked high with the cry.
In this ecstasy at noon
the twelve-year-old brain burns like a motor.

I look ; daylight strolls across noon, lopsided I trudge,
evening piles up a hill on my way.
The wind has moved the grass, but the factory chimneys
    won't budge.
The gold on the river will become gray.

Boy ! Boy ! tomorrow or the day after tomorrow,
this joy in nakedness which is not life's leaven
will be locked up, and the key will be sorrow.
By 1936, a helmet will cover your head instead of a
    heaven.

CZECHOWICZ

Through the Borderlands

The horse lifts its head again and again.
Very monotonously topples the mane :
wheels, the wheels
through fields.

A dreamy half life rattles
along a wood—, a meadow-path,
steep down, down deep
afield.

At dusk, the dark red moon
stumbles over the stubble fields.
Gold leaf !
I weep.

No, there is nothing. No sleep. But the screeching of
    wheels.
The night and its mist are too big for reality.
I weep ; gold leaf.
I weep wheels steep deep afield gold leaf.

CZECHOWICZ

Idyllic Dream

Will the gurgle of rain sound like the snort of a nightmare
as it falls from the low black sky
on the yellow and white, the tinkle of magical flowers?
Ah no. We have the words to conjure with:
sulphur: female horses have woollen manes.

The Virgin Mary walked among the stars,
cooling the souls that smoulder.
Erect in thunder, fearful at midnight, I stood.
O why do you live in that dark corner of dreams? Why keep the
    company of those who sleep?
You ravens, you wolves, you bulky bears, swift stags,
fly. You are free. Do not make us afraid.
Amen.

Purified now by the darkness
your silver comb flashed over the porch.
Speech poured from the quiet ditch
where the voice of sweet sedge
announced the confession of water,
its hands as clean as Mary's stars.

But the orchard is outside, behind the window, (What right have
    we to speak?)
and the useful dill and carrot blossom beyond the beehives.

Purify us too, whoever, wherever, you are:
release us from our own works and from the habits of animals.
We lie like logs on the straw,
but this is why we are kneeling,
and will kneel, still as the dead.

CZECHOWICZ

Grief

My hair is greying but it slants with light
when strands of wind lift it, a chandelier,
that I must always carry through these hollow streets.
The swallows twitter by the river and
it's not so heavy—just my head.
Walk. Walk on.

Walk. Walk. And watch: the scenes, the dreams, the feasts:
cracked glass adorns the synagogues with scars;
a flame gulps up the coarse thick hawser;
the flame of love
denudes us.

The nations are most greedy when they roar.
They cannot whimper like a hungry man.

This evening heavily upon the world
spreads its low length as nostrils scent
red milk from bared volcanoes.
Deciphering which stranger: Who are you?
and multiplying magically through
our own torn selves, I shoot my names, and die.
I die, who huddled with my plough in furrows;
I, a brisk lawyer, drown in instructions;
I, in chlorine, I choking, I dying, gas!
and I am the girl who sleeps with the primrose;
and I, a child, in a live torch, live;
and I at my market stall with the blaze of a bomb;
and I am the madman who's hanged for the fire:
I am my signature, my mother's illiterate cross.

But now the harvest
glows with deep noise.

And how can the river untorture itself and unrust
our brotherly blood before, among us,
the colonnades rise, the mathematical eagles ?
A blizzard of swallows will come
with a whirl that swirls my head,
but through the darkness that the birds give wing
I shall walk, I shall walk on.

Konstanty Ildefons GAŁCZYŃSKI (1905–1953)

The Intelligentsia

We always run away, from town to town,
we—intellectuals :
small and shivering, a tribe without a tribe,
a class of ineffectuals.

From country to country, we shift about with our families :
we each have a gramophone,
millions of us. But it's no use. They keep asking :
"Which country is your own ?"

And since we don't know, we can only weep
oceans of salt oblations.
Beneath fake palms we write artificial letters
and post them in dirty stations.

GAŁCZYŃSKI

Form X. . . .

A numbskull writes to a numbskull, proposing
that he takes the very greatest pleasure in enclosing
Form X. . . .

After great labour and much heart burning
a numbskull takes the very greatest pleasure in returning
Form X. . . .

Tadeusz GAJCY (1922–1944)

Epitaphium

Passer-by, repeat the name
and we shall recognise this place
of day dreaming which carries us
lightly and safely.
The sky grows over our head
and an abandoned distance
clambers up smoke.

Years dozed overhead and they are still there.
Your foot unconsciously
will lift a twig of earth wrapped up in fog
and there'll be such a simple name for lips.
But it's still the same as the voice that strangles the
    throat,
a call from those lonely depths.

You'll not forget, for the water will burn
the proud mouth and the ear of corn will choke.
This country lies in your eyes as an altar
in a grove of smoke would shine like a bone.
You'll cover up your face. Mother's dry hips
will give us no seed, even if after us
a laurel is left as small as a smile,
and history as big as a hand or a heart.

Such is love. It crushes our hands
which have been pierced and laid on the flowers
and the iron as rich as wreaths.
You will not forget, for this love
wrinkles the skin and gives unusual eyes.
You'll see yourself as free beneath a helmet
with our weapon deep in your peaceful dreams.

Stefan BORSUKIEWICZ (1919–1942)

*   *   *

The night was rolling across the plain,
a ball made up of guilt and absolution.
The roads were deep in truth, dragged down from the
    trunks of the willows
and the white trunks of stones.
The wind the confessor spread a bell around.

Once, from raised arms, I created a silence,
and I made a home from the meadows in flower.
I remember, too, living under the shadow of your dream
and the lavender scent of it I recall.

That kind confessor, the wind, spread the bell.

Kazimierz WIERZYŃSKI (1894–1969)

Ballad

The gas-lamps are monks bewitched,
staring empty-eyed.
At night when people sleep,
they take their croziers
and, with their heads bent, stride
along the streets,
their valley of the shadow.
In a long procession
and without a word
they go
to snuff their tapers
in the gas-works yard.

Władysław BRONIEWSKI (1897–1962)

A Word with History

Old Mother History, Queen of Them All,
how you enjoy raising a stink!
Orion peeps through the bars in the wall
and here we sit, you and me, in clink.

You're giving me the same old patter-song
with the same half-derisive leer.
So side by side we go clanking along,
you since Time was, I since last year.

Immortal madam, why and whence
the passion for paradox you display?
Do you really think that it makes sense
to poison the world's blood in this way?

For in the whole wide world I see
nothing but war, conflict and crisis.
Hardly the time, would you agree,
for us to be doing time like this?

Why should a revolutionary poet
rot to death in this Soviet hole?
Dear History, it strikes a jarring note.
Surely one of us is playing the fool?

Shame on you, madam, Queen of Them All ;
let me out of Zamarstynov then.
(And on the other side of the wall
we'll soon be sent down again.)

Aleksander WAT (1900–1967)

Journey

Locked up and bunged in a great empty barrel
deafly I roll down the narrow streets
of this provincial pigsty N***.
The streets are all steep. Not a soul in sight.
True, there are flies. The air black with flies.
Is this what they call night ? How dare they call it night ?
The administration has abolished night.
So no more night in N***,
and no one now will sing "How peaceful are the nights at N***".
The houses show scarcely a gleam at their loopholes.
Vigilance is the rule in this mean town of N***.
Then where, in God's name, is the night watch?
No guard to be seen in this town of the dead.
But how could there be a night watch with no night ?
No pavements, either. A road full of cobbles.
Easy to imagine the boom
rattle
clang
as the barrel rolls down and clambers up.
Uphill—oh, yes—up hill.
This uphill is only the senses' delusion :
The streets of N*** always run down, in fact.
Forever downhill. Down, and that's that. Only down.
No end, you can't see the end, end, end of this down.
The church bells strike for matins, the clock bells for the hour.
The night is now over—night old-style, naturally.
And my black raven stands by the prison gate.

Wojciech BĄK (1907–1961)

Passport

Again they refuse me a passport,
but I will discover a way,
how to sail out of thought, my harbour.
I can always sail out of my thought.

All other countries are welcoming :
no visas, no guards, no customs shed.
The wind has given me giant wings
and there is music against my forehead.

My shadow visits boulevard and slum,
it skips across brisk villages,
each word makes its way to freedom
till a song emerges.

Concord of Leaves

Give me the concord of leaves if you will.
They never ask the wind about their future,
but fall each day more thickly from the maple,
falling into autumn as a sacred pyre.

And if the fire is destined to consume them,
they bow to it, and scurry where it blows
until it blazes. All roads are aflame
with leaves, and the mawkish green of meadows.

The leaves are now as tranquil in this flame
as in the spring when they were flowing first
from clear sap into a green stem.
Serenely they accept the fire and mist.

I love the great tranquility of leaves
that fall into acceptance of their future.
Yes, give me if you will the concord of leaves
in good time—and this pyre.

Stanisław PIĘTAK (1909–1964)

Spells

My old things come to life again,
take pity on me or eye me with contempt.
"You've chosen solitude," they say, "so count on us.
When you fall ill from boredom or despair,
we'll let you see your old house for a moment
and the people you loved there.
You'll even be able to touch them
through the wet tissue of air.
Admit, you didn't want more in life.
You've not much room now, but it will be enough
to kneel in or fall down in,
shouting, cursing, sobbing.
We've taken your pen—but you know how to write
on sand with your finger, in sleep with your moan.
Besides, when dusk begins to thicken
and darkness slowly slides down,
you can almost tap words on the clouds' skin.
Who knows, someone may recognize your sobbing and laughter
on the seventh shore, the seventh star,
and even may echo them."

*   *   *

A leap over years, evading the omens—
for what, but what for ?
To keep the moment of sleep at a distance:
each night it foretells the same end as before.

Not under a blue sky, but on shadow patterns I stand.
No colour feeds my eyes as the sun moves round.
It is almost dark on this familiar ground
whether I go to the cross-roads
or under the plum or the peartree
stand where I snuggled long ago.
On my knees I want to embrace this patch
where the window threw light from my father's house
and played with the dark and the shudder of trees.

Everyone avoids me, no one knows who I am,
so I walk by myself, so I run,
a stranger, believing I must have come
years too early or years too late.

The Sparrow and the Jackdaw

Four miles past Warsaw
a sparrow wed a jackdaw.

They held a celebration.
The owl got no invitation.

The owl came all the same
In style like a great dame.

She settled down—no prig—
And called for a German jig.

A duck could play, a goose jump.
A hen stared like an old frump.

Ortolans, wagtails, thrushes, snipe
danced to the tune of the pipe.

The sparrow was forced to partner the owl
but he bit off her finger—whole.

Crazy sparrow, silly brat,
Why did you bite my thumb like that?

If we were here alone
I'd shake you bone from bone.

Great lady, though you're tall,
I could eat you, feathers and all.

ANONYMOUS

I would sing songs

I would sing songs
If I had my tune.
A cobbler has pinched it
To make four shoon.

Two pairs of shoon
And sold every stitch.
Had I kept my music
I might have been rich.

The Sun sets

The sun as it sets
Looks back tenderly.
Is it midday or twilight
It wants to see ?

It isn't the noon it wants
Or the twilight it wishes to see.
The sun is looking back
At you, just you, Marie.

A Stone

A stone upon a stone,
and on those stones more stones,
and on the topmost stone
another pile of stones.

A stone upon a stone,
and on those stones more stones ;
Write on it, Kate, my dear,
just this, my name, just once.

ANONYMOUS

Near my garden

Near my garden an apple
tree grew rich with sap.

And as its branches spread
its apples turned bright red.

But who will help me pick ?
My Johnny's angry this week.

He got angry, why I don't know—
He came often, why I don't know.

All summer long he came :
I gave him a kiss for shame.

All autumn he came again :
I let him in out of the rain.

All winter he was sad :
I let him into my featherbed.

They're not birds

Beside the lake, this side of it, there stands
A linden tree, a green green tree ;
And on that tree, among its very green,
Three birds will sit—just three.

But they're not birds at all.
They are three gentlemen
Who court a comely girl
—And she will choose which one ?

The first bird says : "You're mine."
The second : "By God's will. . . ."
The third asks : "Darling, comely girl,
What is it makes you mourn ?"

"And why should I not mourn ?
They will wed me to an old man.
He is old and ugly and sluggardly.
He will never be able to hug me."

A new bedroom, a new bed,
A green bed, a deep green bed.
Tell me bedroom, tell me true.
Who'll be the first to sleep in you ?

NOTES

p. 1 ANONYMOUS

LAMENT OF OUR LADY UNDER THE CROSS (*Żale Matki Boskiej pod Krzyżem*), the title is that of editors. The text dates from the middle of the 15th century and is considered to be the best mediaeval poem in Polish, comparable in importance to *Quia amore langueo* in Middle English. Its opening octosyllablic lines give way to a highly complex metre which reaches a dramatic climax in the section beginning with the words "Oh, angel Gabriel." Double and inner rhymes intensify the effect. This dramatic pattern has led to a supposition that the poem is a fragment of an extinct mystery play for Good Friday.

p. 3 ANONYMOUS

FROM EARTHLY DECAY (*Dusza z ciała wyleciała*), a song added to the Wrocław MS. of "The Lament of the Dying Man", dating also from the 15th century. Rhymes and repetitions are closely interwoven.

p. 3 ANONYMOUS

CHARM (*Zarze zarzyce trzy siestrzyce*), a strange piece from the 15th century, probably endowed with some magical purpose. In the translation, "rosie, rosaiden" is an attempt to reproduce both the play on the word *zarze* (meaning the light of dawn) and the inner rhyme, linking *zarzyce* with *siestrzyce* (i.e., sisters).

p. 4 Mikołaj REJ (1505–1569), a nobleman who wrote mainly didactic prose and verse, his most typical collection being "The Mirror" (1568). First attracted to the teaching of Luther, he then turned to Calvinism, but remained all his life essentially a mediaeval moralist.

INDULGENCES, an extract from Rej's dialogue "The Debate between Three Persons, the Squire, the Bailiff and the Parson" (*Krótka rozprawa między trzemi osobami, Panem, Wójtem a Plebanem*, 1543), lines 188–211, spoken by the Squire. The debate ends with the allegorical "Respublica" voicing her overall complaint. Rej's jerky verses are crowded with colloquial phrases and proverbs, which make the text obscure at times.

116

p. 5 Jan KOCHANOWSKI (1530–1584), the most important writer of early Polish literature. Educated in the universities of Cracow, Königsberg and Padua, he became a courtier after his return to Poland, and was later appointed one of the king's secretaries. The death of Sigismund Augustus loosened his ties with the court : Kochanowski settled down in his village Czarnolas, married at the age of forty-five, and as a country squire continued to write. His Polish works include two sets of lyrical *Songs*, the poetic versions of *David's Psalter*, a classical play *The Dismissal of the Greek Envoys*, and the now famous cycle of *Laments*. Among the collections of his Latin verse, *Lyricorum libellus* of 1580 should be singled out.

SONG (*Czego chcesz of nas, Panie*) is believed to be one of Kochanowski's first Polish poems, but was printed c. 1562 together with his conventional piece about Susanna and the elders. Popular tradition maintains that it was written during his stay abroad. The date of the composition, however, cannot be ascertained.

p. 6 LAMENT VIII (*Tren VIII*). The most popular of Kochanowski's laments, in which the expression of grief is poignantly direct. The cycle, first printed in 1580, immortalised the poet's daughter Orszula, who is described in the prose dedication as gracious, delightful and uncommonly gifted. Orszula died when she was only thirty months old (her age is given in Lament XII), probably towards the end of 1579.

p. 6 LAMENT X (*Tren X*). This lament illustrates the way in which Kochanowski mixes mythological allusions with religious and personal beliefs. The last line refers to the forms which apparitions take, and may be compared with Shakespeare's remarks on the nature of ghosts in *Julius Caesar* (IV, 3), or in *Hamlet* (I, 4).

p. 7 IN DEFENCE OF DRUNKARDS (*Za pijanicami*). All through his life Kochanowski wrote light humorous verses, called *fraszki* in Polish (from the Italian *frasca*), which were finally collected in a sumptuous volume (1584). Many of the *fraszki* owed their concepts to classical sources. This, for instance, is an Anacreontic theme, known in other European literatures ; cf. the longer English version by Abraham Cowley, *Drinking*.

p. 7 TO A MATHEMATICIAN (*Na matematyka*). A theme taken from the Greek Anthology.

p. 8   Mikołaj SĘP-SZARZYŃSKI (c. 1550–1581). Little is known of his life. Like Kochanowski he studied abroad. Published posthumously in 1601 by his brother (the volume entitled *Rhythms or Polish Verses*). Sęp-Szarzyński is the best sonneteer in early Polish literature.

ON THESE WORDS OF JOB (*Na one słowa Jopowe*). The quotation taken from the book of Job, ch. XIV, leads to the development of an intricate paradox about man's praise of God.

p. 9   ON THE WAR WE WAGE AGAINST SATAN, THE WORLD AND THE BODY (*O wojnie naszej, którą wiedziemy z Szatanem, światem i ciałem*). The syntax of the original is involved, and play on contrasts resembles the technique of the metaphysical poets. Examples like this made some critics treat Sęp-Szarzyński as a forerunner of the Baroque.

p. 10   Simon SIMONIDES (1558–1629). Of burgher origin, he was made a noble in 1590. He wrote Latin and Polish verse under the penname of Simonides, his best known publication being a volume of idylls, *Sielanki* (1614).

PIETRUCHA'S SONG TO THE SUN is an extract from his idyll "The Reapers" (*Żeńcy*). The idyll presents three characters: the peasant women Pietrucha and Oluchna, and the steward; the setting is a harvest field with the blazing sun overhead. It is to this giver of light, order and love that Pietrucha addresses her songs.

p. 11   Andrzej MORSZTYN (1613 ?–1693). A courtier and statesman who served first King John Casimir Vasa and then John Sobieski. Charged with high treason in 1683, he sought refuge in France, where he died a French citizen. His two collections of poems, *The Dog-star* and *The Lute*, include many translations and adaptations from Marino, but as experiments in language all are outstanding. Morsztyn also translated Corneille's *Le Cid*, which was performed in Warsaw (1662).

TO ST. JOHN THE BAPTIST (*Do S. Jana Babtisti*). Verses 5–6 allude to Zacharias's dumbness.

p. 12   ON LITTLE FLIES : A SONG (*Na muszki pieśń*). From the MS. in the Radziwiłł archives; printed in 1949. For analogous effect produced by a startling concept, cf. Donne's *The Flea*.

p. 13 SONG (*Pieśń: Kasiu, czyś chora*). The poem refers to the siege of Toruń in 1658. The city was occupied by the Swedes during their invasion of Poland. Morsztyn stayed in the camp with King John Casimir. The Kate of the poem was probably Catherine Gordon, a lady of Scottish origin attached to the court, whom Morsztyn married in 1659.

p. 14 Zbigniew MORSZTYN (1620 ?–1690 ?), a courtier and soldier who served the Radziwiłł family. During the Swedish invasion in 1655, however, he remained loyal to King John Casimir, fought the enemy, was-wounded and taken prisoner. When an edict was passed after the Swedish war, expelling the Arians from Poland, Morsztyn adhered to his religious beliefs and chose exile in the principality of Prussia. Like the poetry of the other Morsztyn, Zbigniew's works circulated in manuscripts. His most comprehensive MS. collection is *The Homely Muse*.

EMBLEM 39 (*Emblema 39*). From Morsztyn's cycle of religious poems, *Emblemata*. The cycle was probably composed while the poet lived in exile. It contains one hundred and thirteen poems, and is dedicated to Princess Catherine Radziwiłł born Sobieska, sister of King John III and a zealous Catholic in her later years. A note preceding the text explains that the brief inscriptions above the poems, upon which the Princess wished to have Polish verses composed, were written by "a certain Capuchin". The note further alludes to a collection of pictorial emblems, which has only just been identified.

p. 15 EMBLEM 51 (*Emblema 51*). Like the previous emblem, this is written in eleven-syllable lines, rhymed *aa, bb*. In my opinion *Emblem 51* shows Morsztyn's style at its best.

p. 16 Samuel TWARDOWSKI (1600–1660). A humble country squire born in Western Poland and educated by the Jesuits, won literary fame during his lifetime as "the Polish Virgil". This reputation rested chiefly on his two long epic poems, *Władysław IV* and *The Civil War*. Nowadays he is more appreciated for his pastoral poem, *The Comely Pasqualine*, which reveals the subtlety of Twardowski's diction.

THE SULTAN AT THE MOSQUE, a passage from "The Most Important Embassy of the Illustrious Prince Christopher Zbaraski . . . to

Mustafa, the Most Mighty Sultan of the Turkish Empire, in the year 1621" (*Przeważna legacja J.O. Ks. Krzysztofa Zbaraskiego . . . do najpotężniejszego cesarza tureckiego Mustafy w r. 1621*, published 1633). The young poet accompanied his patron, Prince Zbaraski, on his embassy to Constantinople, and recorded in verse their journey across the Balkan lands and their stay at the exotic capital. The result is, in fact, a literary mixture, partly a travel book, partly a panegyrical memoir, but the observed scenes have retained odd charm.

p. 17 CUPID'S SUICIDE, an extract from Point III of the pastoral romance "The Comely Pasqualine" (*Nadobna Pasqualina*, 1655). This is a story about Pasqualine's rivalry with Venus and her perilous pilgrimage to Juno's temple, where she is purified of all worldly desires. On her return to Lisbon, Pasqualine turns her palace into a cloister. Thus defeated, Venus has to flee in shame, while her son Cupid, tricked out of his bow and arrows, commits suicide. In the end the poem becomes a denunciation of pastoral licence and a praise of divine love. Stylistically, it is the best exposition of the baroque technique in both its narrative and lyrical manner. Throughout the poem Twardowski contrasts words of Slavonic and Latin origin, producing a truly Romance atmosphere. *The Comely Pasqualine* is supposedly based on an unknown Spanish source: "from the Spanish, attired in Polish dress", as the title says. Cupid's suicide certainly adds a puzzling novelty to the pastoral formula.

p. 18 EPITAPH FOR A DOG (*Nagrobek Garsonkowi*). This epitaph follows an elegy on the death of a certain Jacob Wojewódzki, killed at Smolensk. It is, I think, one of the most effective 17th-century poems, in which the knowledge of animal behaviour equals the poetic self-assurance.

p. 19 Wacław POTOCKI (1625–1696), a country squire who had to abandon Arianism after the Swedish–Polish war during which, like many of his co-religionists, he at first supported the enemy. He wrote a great deal, but what was printed in his lifetime did not represent his best manner of writing. Now he is recognised chiefly for his epic poem *The Chocim War*, and a bulky collection of occasional verse in the *fraszka* tradition. Potocki's literature, though very uneven, retains its social value, because it mirrors the life of the Polish gentry at a time of political and religious conflicts.

WINTER, BEFORE THE WAR, an extract from Part II of "The Chocim War" (*Transakcyja wojny chocimskiej*). This long poem, divided into ten parts, describes the Turkish attack on Poland in 1621, which was successfully repulsed at Chocim on the Dniester river. Potocki based his poetic account on contemporary sources, especially on Jacob Sobieski's Latin memoirs, *Commentariorum belli Chotinensis libri tres* (1646). Completed in 1670, the poem remained in manuscript until 1850, when it was first printed, but wrongly ascribed to Andrzej Lipski.

p. 20 THE TURKISH ARMY, an extract from Part IV of "The Chocim War" (*Transakcyja wojny chocimskiej*). The Turkish Emperor, Osman II, led an army of (according to chroniclers) over two hundred thousand men against Poland, and it was composed of diverse races and nations. The poet exploits the possibilities of his exotic subject and crowds the lines with foreign-sounding names. This gives a strange musical effect, not unlike that of Milton in *Paradise Lost*, Book I, where we find a similar accumulation of names (e.g., lines 340–425). Potocki's model could have been *The Acts of the Apostles*, ch. II, 9–11 ("Cappadocia, in Pontus . . . Phrygia, and Pamphylia . . .").

p. 21 Bartłomiej ZIMOROWIC (1597–c. 1680), of burgher origin, reached a prominent position in the city of Lvov. His Latin works are now completely overshadowed by his Polish idylls, collected in the volume of 1663. As Zimorowic published his poetry under the name of his younger brother Szymon (who died at the age of twenty-one), the authorship of the volume entitled *Roxolanki* (1654) is still disputed. Modern scholars have no doubt about the idylls being the work of Bartłomiej, and one cannot see any reason why the myth of the youthful Szymon should be preserved for the other volume.

JUDGMENT DAY is a passage from the idyll "The Anniversary" (*Roczyzna*) included in the volume "The New Ruthenian Idylls" (*Sielanki nowe ruskie*, 1663). It exemplifies the baroque grandeur of Zimorowic's themes. Unfortunately, the best of his Ruthenian idylls are too long to be translated in their entirety.

p. 22 AGAINST BAD VERSIFIERS is an ironic digression taken from "The Vine-dressers" (*Winiarze*) in the volume *The New Ruthenian Idylls*. The goat's tail is here twisted in more senses than one.

p. 23 QUERIES, again this is a passage from "The Vine-dressers" (*Winiarze*), perhaps the most moving lyrical statement to be found in Polish baroque verse.

p. 24 IN MOTION, a fragment of the idyll "The Bride goes to her new home" (*Przenosiny*), which has a few local touches. The lines here are shorter (eleven syllables), and the whole effect aims at giving a sensation of movement.

p. 24 THE POET'S RHYMES, an extract from "The Bandore-Players" (*Kobeźnicy*), another quotable idyll in the 1663 volume. Zimorowic, as conscious of the struggle with style as most inventive artists, liked to make allusions to his poetic tools.

p. 25 EPITAPH. These are the last four lines of "The Weepers" (*Narzekalnice*), a poem typical for its strict observance of the idyll form. The epitaph in the original has no verbs at all, the nouns facing one another in direct contrast.

p. 26 Ignacy KRASICKI (1735–1801), the representative 18th-century writer, and friend of the last king of Poland. He had a brilliant career in the Church as prince bishop of Warmia and finally as archbishop of Gniezno. After the first partition he became a subject of Frederick the Great of Prussia, but unlike Voltaire managed to make his stays at court quite amiable. Krasicki died and was buried in Berlin. His versatile talent led him into a number of *genres*, but in the fables and satires he expressed the deeper moods of his moderately sceptical character. He also tried his hand at mock-heroic verse and a novel, the latter of which —because of its early date, 1776—is now regarded as a classic in Polish letters.

THE LAMB AND THE WOLVES (*Jagnię i wilcy*) from the volume "Fables and Parables" (*Bajki i przypowieści*), published in 1779. This collection, which fully justifies Krasicki's fame as a stylist and wit, contains epigrammatic poems, some of them only four lines long, and is distinguished by the use of dialogue in very compact structures.

p. 26 CAGED BIRDS (*Ptaszki w klatce*) from *Fables and Parables*, 1779. Printed seven years after the first partition of Poland, this poem was a discreet yet painful reminder of political realities.

p. 26 THE MASTER AND THE DOG (*Pan i pies*), again from the volume of 1779.

p. 27 THE HERON, THE FISH AND THE CRAB (*Czapla, ryby i rak*). This is a celebrated poem from the collection "New Fables" (*Bajki nowe*), published after Krasicki's death in the complete edition of his works (1802–1804). *New Fables*, in contrast to the volume of 1779, contains more elaborate narrative pieces in which varied lines, short and long, are further enlivened by clever rhymes.

p. 28 Franciszek ZABŁOCKI (1754–1821). Wrote many comedies modelled on the French theatre, and coloured them with local observations and allusions. His satirical verse has the sharpness of political invective.

DENUNCIATION (*Doniesienie*) dates from the period when Zabłocki was engaged in defending the patriotic reforms which were discussed at the Four-Year Diet (1788–1792). In anonymous leaflets he attacked those especially who were in Russian pay.

p. 29 Franciszek KARPIŃSKI (1741–1825), an impoverished nobleman from the south-east borders, educated at the Jesuit academy in Lvov; became famous for his pastoral love songs but failed to secure any permanent literary patronage. At the end of his long life he wrote a book of memoirs, notable for its frank tone and vivid prose.

RECOLLECTION OF PAST LOVE (*Przypomnienie dawnej miłości*) is undoubtedly Karpiński's best poem. It belongs to the group in which Justyna's name occurs. Karpiński's love for this girl is also described in his memoirs, but with a realistic touch of common sense.

p. 31 LETTER OF EXCUSE (*List wymawiający się*) shows Karpiński in his casual manner. Tsar Peter, referred to in the third stanza, died in 1725.

p. 32 Franciszek Dionizy KNIAŹNIN (1750–1807), poet and translator of Horace, attached to the court of Prince Czartoryski at Puławy; was interested in both folklore and contemporary science. He himself supervised the complete edition of his poetic works (1787–1788). Inclined towards moods of melancholy, Kniaźnin's mind could not bear the tragedy of the last partition, and dark years of madness followed.

COMPOSED DURING A JOURNEY (*Z podróży*). In the original some of the place-names occur in rhymes, adding yet another effect to the ingenious structure of the poem.

p. 34 TO WHISKERS (*Do wąsów*). One of the most popular of 18th-century poems. Kniaźnin wrote it in several versions: this one dates from 1787. Czarnecki, mentioned in the fourth stanza, led the army which chased the Swedes out of Poland in the 17th century.

p. 35 Julian NIEMCEWICZ (1757–1841), deputy at the Four-Year Diet, playwright, poet, novelist and translator. He was taken prisoner with General Kościuszko after the defeat at Maciejowice (1794) and spent a year and a half in a Russian fortress. When Tsar Paul gave Kościuszko his freedom, Niemcewicz accompanied him on his triumphant journey via England to the United States. There Niemcewicz married an American lady, but in 1807 he returned to Poland and resumed his literary career. The rising of 1830 made him an exile once more, and he died in Paris. He knew English well and translated Dryden, Milton, Pope, Gray, Samuel Johnson, Wordsworth and others (*Rasselas* and *The Rape of the Lock* in particular, soothed the boredom of his imprisonment). He enjoyed his five visits to England (the first as early as 1784), and when sent on a diplomatic mission in 1831, he kept a remarkable record of his impressions in a diary.

WRITTEN ON THE COACH-BOX BETWEEN CHELTENHAM AND LONDON, SEPTEMBER 24th, 1832. Entered in Niemcewicz's diary from the years 1831–33. This informal piece, hurriedly jotted down, was written by a man of seventy-five. It does not amount to much as poetry, but is a proof of Niemcewicz's mental agility. The poet himself commented: "One can see that these rhymes were written on a coach-box."

p. 36 Antoni MALCZEWSKI (1793–1826). His short life was fairly dramatic: he served in the army, travelled abroad, conquered the peak of Mont Blanc in 1818, but after his return to Poland formed a disastrous liaison with a mentally unbalanced woman, whom he tried to cure with the help of fashionable magnetism. The publication of his *Maria* was ignored, but the poem received due appreciation four years after Malczewski's death, when the Romantic critic, Mochnacki, used it to illustrate and justify the new movement.

OPEN SPACES, an extract from *Maria*, Canto I, 8. The poem, first published in 1825, has the subtitle: "an Ukrainian tale". The plot centres round Maria who by secretly marrying Wacław, rouses the vengeful anger of his father, a powerful magnate.

p. 37 AFTER THE BATTLE is a passage from the second Canto of *Maria* (section 13).

p. 38 THE WINDOW CURTAIN is the most dramatic sequence from the end of *Maria* (Canto II, 15 and 16). It describes Wacław's return after the victorious battle with the Tartars to the home of his wife Maria. He finds her dead.

p. 39 Adam MICKIEWICZ (1798–1855), a native of the Nowogródek district in the Lithuanian part of Poland, was educated in the University of Vilna, then a flourishing centre of learning. There he published his first volume of ballads and romances in the Romantic style (1822). Though he was already a secondary school teacher, he became implicated in the trial of Vilna students (1823), and as a result was deported to Russia, where, however, he enjoyed many social and literary successes. Allowed to leave Russia, he travelled through Germany and Italy and finally settled in Paris. The November rising of 1830 decided his status as a political exile for life. From 1840 to 1844 he lectured on Slavonic literatures at the Collège de France. During the Crimean War Mickiewicz went on a mission to the Polish legion in Turkey, but soon died in Constantinople.

THE GUESTS (*Do wizytujących*), a love sonnet from his volume *Sonety*, first published in Moscow, 1826.

p. 40 BAJDARY (*Bajdary*), from the cycle of "Crimean Sonnets" (*Sonety krymskie*) included in the volume of 1826. Bajdary: a valley leading to the southern shore of Crimea. The poet visited the peninsula in the company of his friends.

p. 41 THE PRISONER'S RETURN is a passage from a long monologue in Mickiewicz's play "The Ancestors" (*Dziady*), Part III, scene vii. Part III, written at Dresden in 1832, is based on the poet's experiences during the Vilna trial. In scene vii, against the smart background of a Warsaw salon, an arrival from Vilna describes the political terror inflicted by the Russians on the Lithuanian provinces.

p. 43 INNER MONOLOGUE, from Book V of *Pan Tadeusz* (1834). Telimena, an ageing lady, is oddly misplaced in the provincial atmosphere of Soplicowo : she dreams of her past social successes in St. Petersburg, but also considers the situation close at hand, which involves two elegible bachelors : the Count and Tadeusz.

p. 45 OVER THE GREAT CLEAR POOL (*Nad wodą wielką i czystą*), one of Mickiewicz's late lyrics written during his stay at Lausanne, 1839–1840.

p. 46 Juliusz SŁOWACKI (1809–1849), son of a university professor, educated in Vilna, worked for a time as a civil servant in Warsaw where he witnessed the outbreak of the November rising. Left Poland a few months later, travelled to England as a courier in 1831, stayed in Switzerland for a time, but then lived mostly in Paris which was the centre of Polish émigrés. There he published, at his own expense, plays and volumes of poems. His letters to his mother, spanning the years of his exile, form the chief biographical source, and have also become classics of Polish prose.

HYMN (*Hymn*), written 19 October 1836, at the beginning of Słowacki's journey to the Middle East, which he undertook with two friends. The experiences of this journey are reflected in a number of Słowacki's works.

p. 48 A CAROL, sung in Słowacki's play *Złota Czaszka*, Act I, scene 3 (1842). The inclusion of Latin and the use of diminutives help to re-create the traditional form.

p. 49 GIVE ME A MILE OF LAND (*Dajcie mi tylko jedną ziemi milę*). First printed posthumously in 1882.

p. 50. FAREWELL (*Bo to jest wieszcza najjaśniejsza chwała*), written in 1848, published posthumously in 1879.

p. 50 THAT ANGEL BURNING AT MY LEFT SIDE (*Anioł ognisty—mój anioł lewy*), represents the mystical period of Słowacki's writing. It was published posthumously in 1881.

p. 51 Zygmunt KRASIŃSKI (1812–1859), came from a wealthy aristocratic family. His life was dominated by the personality of his father, who became a loyal supporter of the Russian rule. Out of this conflict and a sense of guilt grew Krasiński's literature, both patriotic and prophetic, but always hidden under a veil of anonymity. Free to travel in Europe, Krasiński met the émigré poets, published his books abroad, and continued his uncomfortable existence as a writer. His great intellectual abilities led him towards philosophic concepts. In his prose play, "The Undivine Comedy" (1835), he envisaged the class conflict of the future, and its bold structure is still impressive as theatre. One of Krasiński's friends, with whom he corresponded, was an English publicist, Henry Reeve.

GOD HAS DENIED ME THE ANGELIC MEASURE (*Bóg mi odmówił tej anielskiej miary*). Date: 7 July 1836. Krasiński was acutely aware of the limitations of his poetic technique and he certainly wrote far better prose than verse. This is a moving confession of failure, which by way of contrast becomes a successful poem on its own terms.

p. 52 Cyprian NORWID (1821–1883) was haunted by poverty all his life. He lost his parents early and received little formal education. The years of his youth in Warsaw were oppressed by the atmosphere of defeat after the rising of 1830, but he made a name for himself as a poet. Allowed to travel abroad in 1842, he studied sculpture for a short time in Italy and then decided to become a voluntary exile. Norwid was befriended in Paris by Chopin and some of the émigré writers, tried to improve his fortune in America (1852), but returned, disappointed and penniless, to Paris, where he finally died in 1883, at a home for impoverished Polish exiles. A few years later his remains were transferred to a communal grave. Ignored and even ridiculed by his contemporaries, Norwid was re-discovered by Przesmycki, a poet and critic, at the beginning of our century. From that time on, Norwid's poetry has been edited and studied by many modern critics who see in him not only the most important innovator of Polish poetic diction in the 19th century, but also a profoundly original mind whose impact on Polish literature will be felt by many generations to come.

CONVERSATION PIECE. This is the opening passage from Norwid's *Promethidion*, an unconventional poetic dialogue about the ultimate meaning of art, labour, beauty and love. It was published "under the author's imprint" in Paris (1851), two years after Chopin's death. Although its metre observes a syllabic regularity (eleven syllables), it is moulded on the rhythms of common speech. Judging by Norwid's note to his preface, he himself intended the verse of *Promethidion* "to draw not too much attention with its colloquial flow". Later he developed the colloquialism of his syllabic metres into free verse proper. In this respect Norwid's metrical experiments bring him nearer to the poetry of Browning, Laforgue and Pound. The words in italics are meant to indicate the emphasis of voice.

p. 54   THOSE WHO LOVE. Like the previous piece, this extract is taken from the first part of *Promethidion*, entitled *Bogumił* after one of the speakers. Deeply interested in native folklore, Norwid had this in common with Chopin that he was never sentimental about it. He well knew the distorting influence of the partitions on the country's popular culture. Before he left Poland, Norwid as a very young man had twice made long excursions on foot into the Polish countryside, and later relied on those memories in exile.

p. 54   BUT JUST TO SEE, another extract from the first part of *Promethidion*, significant for its functional interpretation of art within the national context.

p. 55   FATE (*Fatum*), a poem from the collection *Vade-mecum* (1866), which Norwid intended as a guide to new poetry, though he could not find a publisher for it. The incomplete MS. was reproduced by a photo-typed process in 1947.

p. 56   THE METROPOLIS (*Stolica*), from the collection *Vade-mecum*. This is Paris in the 1860s. Norwid reacted against the landscape poetry of the Romantics and often used urban motifs with an ironic skill. The lines here are irregular, though the stanza pattern is preserved in rhymes.

p. 57   RECIPE FOR A WARSAW NOVEL (*Przepis na powieść warszawską*). Norwid also practised the traditional *fraszka* type of verse and has left a number of such lucid and witty invectives.

p. 58   SEQUENCE FROM A POEM. This is taken from the experimental poem *A Dorio ad Phrygium* (c. 1872), in which Norwid dispensed with nearly all rhymes and gave his free rhythms a wider narrative scope.

p. 60   Władysław SYROKOMLA (1823–1862) is the pen-name of Ludwik Kondratowicz who lived near Vilna in eastern Poland. He worked for a few years as a clerk on the estate of Prince Radziwiłł; then tried farming on lease, but without success. Forced by constant financial insecurity to earn a living from books, he wrote and published much, his verse tales enjoying considerable popularity. At his most inspired, Syrokomla drew on regional and idyllic themes, but on occasions he could use a sharper pen in social or patriotic protest. Syrokomla is now underrated in criticism, but his lyrical poetry may well be due for revival.

THE RAVEN (*Kruk*) is a song based on the Lithuanian version of a well-known ballad theme. It belongs to a group of Syrokomla's songs written to the music of W. Każyński. Launched in this way, *The Raven* became very popular.

p. 61   FROM THE MADHOUSE, the first section from the cycle *Melodie z domu obłąkanych*, written during the moods of depression towards the very end of the poet's life. This is perhaps the most original work left by Syrokomla.

p. 62   EPITAPH FOR A COUNTRY SQUIRE (*Nagrobek obywatelowi*) represents the satirical manner of Syrokomla. It dates from 1861, a year of political disturbances in Poland, when the poet was confined by the Russian authorities to his village home and could not visit Vilna.

p. 63   Adam ASNYK (1838–1897), well educated in Poland and Germany, took part in political conspiracies, was appointed member of the revolutionary National Government in 1863, but after the collapse of the insurrection had to live in the Austrian part of Poland where he published books of lyrical verse and dramas. Once highly appreciated as a poet, especially for his philosophical sonnets, *Over the Depths*, he is now suffering an eclipse in literary reputation.

GREY HORSE (*Siwy koniu*) is included in the cycle *From Peasant Motifs*. These stylised poems in the popular manner have retained their freshness.

p. 64   Maria KONOPNICKA (1842–1910) was a prolific writer of verse, but its high-minded tone makes her now almost unreadable. She even attempted a huge epic poem about Polish peasant settlers in Brazil, all fitted neatly into the *ottava rima*. Today Konopnicka is remembered as a writer of short stories and admired for her extraordinary book for children about the orphan girl Marysia and the dwarfs.

A VISION (*Wizja*). "Emptiness, white and endless" is probably an allusion to Siberia. Treated as a symbol in order to evade political censorship, the subject of the poem gains in poetic quality.

p. 65 Stanisław WYSPIAŃSKI (1869–1907), dramatist and painter whose creative work was connected with the city of Cracow. He married a peasant woman and described another wedding of an intellectual friend with a peasant woman in his great play *Wesele*. His poetic theatre which in many ways continues the Polish Romantic tradition, is formally close to Symbolism. Another characteristic seems to be the blend of themes from Polish history and Greek mythology. Considering the brevity of his life and his tragic illness, Wyspiański has left a large body of work, but few of his plays are comparable in artistic quality with *Wesele*.

THE POET AND THE PEASANT BRIDE, a sequence from Act III, scene 16, of "The Wedding" (*Wesele*), 1901. The metre is a conscious imitation of peasant doggerel as used in Nativity plays.

p. 67 LET NOBODY WEEP OVER MY GRAVE (*Niech nikt nad grobem mi nie płacze*). The poem was written in July, 1903. Depressive moods recurred during Wyspiański's illness and brought out this kind of bitterness. He died of syphilis.

p. 68 HOW CAN I CALM MYSELF (*Jakżeż ja się uspokoję*). From Wyspiański's posthumous MSS.

p. 69 Lucjan RYDEL (1870–1918), son of a university professor, had a great theatrical success with his "Enchanted Circle". His marriage to a peasant girl from Bronowice gave Wyspiański the dramatic concept of *The Wedding*. In the play he is represented as The Bridegroom. Once a popular writer, Rydel has been much neglected in recent years.

THE RAINBOW (the opening line in Polish: *Od Krakowa czarny las*) is taken from Rydel's cycle "To My Wife" (*Żonie mojej*, 1901) which often recaptures the charm and manner of peasant songs from the Cracow district.

p. 70   Kazimierz TETMAJER (1865–1940), born in the mountain region of Podhale which he later depicted in a set of excellent short stories. His lyrical poems, modishly decadent, enjoyed great popularity at the turn of the century. A brain disease, however, stopped his literary activities, and in the period between the wars Tetmajer existed like a shadow of his fame. During the German occupation of Warsaw he was found unconscious in a snowdrift and died the same night.

IN THE SISTINE CHAPEL (*W Kaplicy Sykstyńskiej*). Tetmajer is at his best, not in the poetic atmospherics for which he was famous, but in brief descriptive pieces like this record of impressions.

p. 71   Tadeusz MICIŃSKI (1873–1919), a poet and author of a few mystical novels and dramas ; was murdered by peasants in Soviet White Russia.

GOOD-BYE (*Bądź zdrowa !*). This elusive poem from the volume *In the Twilight of Stars* (1902) has become a favourite anthology piece.

p. 72   Jan KASPROWICZ (1860–1926), the first great poet of peasant origin, born in the village of Szymborze in Kuyavia. Studied first in Germany, then completed his education himself, and eventually gained a professorship in comparative literature. His best volumes of poetry are : *Poems* (1889), *To the Perishing World* (1902), *The Ballad of the Sunflower* (1908), *The Book of the Poor* (1916) and *My World* (1926). Kasprowicz also translated a great deal from Greek, German and especially from English. His mystery play *Marcholt* (1920), written over many years, has much topicality hidden under its grotesque concept.

THE SUNSET is a passage from Kasprowicz's most famous hymn "My Evening Song" (*Moja pieśń wieczorna*), printed in the volume of 1902. As this poem is over four hundred lines long, it cannot be included here in its entirety. In all his hymns Kasprowicz experimented not only with free verse, but also with the musical pattern of motifs. This is one such sequence, illuminating his technique. *My Evening Song* was written in a cottage facing the Tatra mountains.

p. 74   LANDSCAPE ON THE MOVE is again an extract from a long poem, "Holy God, Holy and Mighty". (*Święty Boże, święty, mocny*). The title is that of a penitential hymn sung in Polish churches.

Kasprowicz himself admitted that the images of his village childhood imprinted themselves on his hymns. *Holy God, Holy and Mighty* also appeared in the volume *To the Perishing World*, 1902.

p. 76 THE BALLAD OF THE SUNFLOWER (*Ballada o słoneczniku*) from the volume of the same title, published in 1908. This is, beyond any doubt, one of the best poems in the language.

p. 79 THE DAY BEFORE HARVEST (*Dzień przedżniwny*), a representative poem from Kasprowicz's last volume, "My World" (*Mój świat*, 1926). "Mr. Godlord" corresponds to the peasant compound *Panbóg*. "Davidson" replaces the surname *Zakrętowy* in the original. The volume abounds in proper names and local detail.

p. 81 Edward SŁOŃSKI (1874–1926), a poet who earned his living as a dentist; acquired some fame for the patriotic poems he wrote during the first world war.

SHE WHO HAS NOT DIED (*Ta, co nie zginęła*). The title alludes to the first line of the national anthem. Written after the outbreak of the war, it was published in the volume of 1915, also entitled *Ta, co nie zginęła*. Poles had to fight against one another in the armies of their foreign rulers.

p. 83 Bolesław LEŚMIAN (1879–1937), a symbolist poet of Jewish origin (his name was Lesman), educated in Kiev, wrote some of his early poems in Russian. His volume *The Meadow* (1920) confirmed his reputation as an original writer: he became, in fact, the poets' poet. Leśmian practised law in a provincial town, and towards the end of his life was elected member of The Polish Academy of Literature.

IN THE DARK (*Po ciemku*), from the volume "A Drink of Shades" (*Napój cienisty*, 1936), the last published in his lifetime.

p. 84 BROTHER (*Brat*). From the same volume of 1936.

p. 85 THE CEMETERY (*Cmentarz*), again from the volume *A Drink of Shades*.

p. 86 MEMORIES (*Wspomnienie*). As above.

p. 88 Leopold STAFF (1878–1957), a prolific but minor poet, also a dramatist and translator; published his first volume in the year of Wyspiański's *Wesele*, and kept on writing into his old age.

THE FOUNTAIN (*Fontanna*), from one of his later volumes, "The Colour of Honey" (*Barwa miodu*, 1936).

p. 89 Emil ZEGADŁOWICZ (1888–1941), belonged to a group of poets who cultivated regionalism with a somewhat self-conscious zeal. He also wrote much devotional verse, but later shocked his public with daring semi-autobiographical novels, and changed over from pious to Red propaganda.

THE VAGABOND CROSSES (*O krzyżach łazęgach*), from his volume *Kolędziołki beskidzkie* (1923), whose title is impossible to translate. Lines 13–15: *Kalwaria* and *Alwernia*, two small towns in Southern Poland.

p. 90 Tytus CZYŻEWSKI (1885–1945), a Futurist poet and a painter of the Formist movement, much underrated in official criticism. His early poetry successfully resisted the urban tendencies in Futurism by treating folklore in an experimental way.

SPRING, 1917 (*Wiosna 1917 r.*), one of Czyżewski's later poems (1936). Kostrowicki was the Polish name of the poet Apollinaire.

p. 91 Julian TUWIM (1894–1953), a very popular poet between the two wars, was born of Jewish parents in the industrial town of Lodz, and later lived in Warsaw. He had wide antiquarian interests, contributed light verses and songs to fashionable cabarets and was a skilful translator of Russian poetry. Tuwim spent the war years in America, but on his return to Poland in 1946 became a loyal supporter of the Stalinist regime.

WIFE (*Żona*), from the volume "The Seventh Autumn" (*Siódma jesień*, 1921).

p. 92 Maria PAWLIKOWSKA (1895–1945), a poetess renowned for her epigrammatic verses; also wrote a number of fashionable plays. She died in exile, in England.

133

OCTOBER (*Październik*) from the volume "Kisses" (*Pocałunki*, 1926).

p. 93 Jan LECHOŃ (1899–1956), a poet who joined the diplomatic service, later to become an exile. He began writing as a very young man, but in his mature years published very little. His life in New York ended in suicide.

ON THE DEATH OF JOSEPH CONRAD (*Na śmierć Józefa Conrada*), from the volume of 1942, published in London. Conrad's father, Apollo Korzeniowski, was buried in Cracow, in 1869.

p. 94 Stanisław MŁODOŻENIEC (1895–1959), a Futurist poet of peasant origin, was a teacher in a secondary school. After the war he lived in London, but returned to Poland a short time before his death.

MOSCOW (*Moskwa*), a Futurist classic from the volume of 1921, entitled with characteristic nonchalance "Dashes and Futuresques" (*Kreski i futureski*). The poem is about the ringing bells of Moscow.

p. 95 Józef CZECHOWICZ (1903–1939), a representative poet of the *avant-garde* movement, born in Lublin; worked first as a village teacher, then as an editor on a children's weekly. At the very beginning of the war he was killed during an air-raid on his native town.

BRAIN 12 YEARS OLD (*mózg lat 12*), from the volume *A Day as Everyday*, 1930. The original text, like all Czechowicz's poems, has neither punctuation nor capital letters.

p. 97 THROUGH THE BORDERLANDS (*przez kresy*), from the volume *A Ballad from the Other Side*, 1932. The whole poem is based on musical effects.

p. 98 IDYLLIC DREAM (*sen sielski*), from Czechowicz's last volume, *The Human Clef*, 1939.

p. 99 GRIEF (*żal*). Written in 1938, it appeared in Czechowicz's last volume.

p. 101 Konstanty Ildefons GAŁCZYŃSKI (1905–1953), a born anarchist among modern poets, who treated extreme political ideas as props in his private circus of life, and swung from right to left, becoming in the end the oddest of propagandists in the "People's Republic". His early lyrical poems and his grotesque fantasies are filled with genuine inspiration.

THE INTELLIGENTSIA (The first line in Polish: *Wciąż uciekamy. Z miasta do miasta.*) First printed in 1936.

p. 102   FORM X. . . . (*Droga służbowa*). No. 8 in a short cycle *Grüssen aus Polen* (1935).

p. 103   Tadeusz GAJCY (1922–1944), began to write poetry during the years of occupation; was killed in the Warsaw Rising on 14 August, 1944.

EPITAPHIUM (*Epitafium*). Though confused in structure, this poem has a precise tone of authority.

p. 104   Stefan BORSUKIEWICZ (1919–1942), born in Western Poland, one of the most gifted poets who began writing during the last war. He died as the result of a fatal accident while training with the Polish parachute brigade in Scotland.

* * *   From Borsukiewicz's only volume of verse "Contrasts" (*Kontrasty*), published in London in 1941.

p. 105   Kazimierz WIERZYŃSKI (1894–1969), in his early poems praised youth and physical prowess. At the Olympics of 1928 his *Laur olimpijski* was awarded a literary prize. Later, Wierzyński assumed a bardic role which was intensified and made personal by the experience of exile.

BALLAD   (*Ballada*), from Wierzyński's second book "Sparrows on the Roof" (*Wróble na dachu*, 1920), a miniature remarkable for its well-developed image. Line 11: "tapers" (*gromnice*), lit in the hour of death.

p. 106   Władysław BRONIEWSKI (1897–1962), a poet involved in politics, his verse oscillating between revolutionary rhetoric and sentimental lyricism (as in "The Care and the Song", *Troska i pieśń*, 1932). He was both a patriot proud of his military record in the Polish–

Russian war of 1920, and a communist critical of a free Poland. After the Stalin–Hitler pact he was ideologically rewarded with several months in Soviet prisons. Released in 1941, he joined General Anders's army, wrote more patriotic poems, but a few years later returned to Poland where he soon became an official Party poet, and crowned this masochistic achievement with "The Lay of Stalin" (*Słowo o Stalinie*, 1950). There he piously intoned :

> Glory to the name of Stalin !
> Peace to the world, peace . . .

A WORD WITH HISTORY (*Rozmowa z Historią*), from the volume *Wiersze*, published posthumously in Paris (1962). Last stanza, line 2 : Zamarstinov (*Zamarstynów*), a suburb in Lvov with a jail, in which Broniewski was put by the Soviet occupants. The poem has a few slang expressions about "doing time", such as *na kiblu*, which literally means "sitting on a prison bucket". This ironic piece from 1940 should be contrasted with the lines in the poem "Hope" (*Nadzieja*, 1951):

> It's beautiful to think that in Moscow
> Stalin lives.
> It's beautiful to think that in Moscow
> Stalin thinks [etc.]

107 Aleksander WAT (Aleksander Chwat, 1900–1967), a self-conscious Futurist in his youth, used teasing titles like "I from this side and I from the other side of my puggy-iron stove" (1920), but after imprisonment in Soviet Russia and during a long illness he found a new poetic voice. Wat left Poland in 1959 and died in France.

JOURNEY (*Podróż*), from the volume "Verses" (*Wiersze*, 1957), an intriguing example of Wat's later manner.

p. 108 Wojciech BĄK (1907–1961), an essentially religious poet from western Poland, his reputation was established in 1934 with the book "The Burden of Heaven" (*Brzemię niebieskie*). After surviving the German occupation, Bąk faced persecution from the communist regime, which drove him to a lunatic asylum where, however, he continued to write verse.

PASSPORT (the first line in Polish : *Gdy odmówiono mi paszportu*), from "Congealed Moments" (*Zastygłe chwile*, 1958). It is said that during his stay in a mental home Bąk would now and again apply for a passport. This request was treated as a sign of madness.

CONCORD OF LEAVES (the first line is Polish : *Jeżeli zechcesz, daj mi zgodę liści*), from the cycle "Song above Madness" (*Śpiew ponad obłędem*), which forms the first part of the volume "Congealed Moments".

p. 110   Stanisław PIĘTAK (1909–1964), a poet of peasant origin from the Sandomierz district, who experimented with narrative verse and owed much to the pastoral tradition. After the war his lyrical poems became increasingly disturbed and he committed suicide.

SPELLS (*Zaklinania*), from the volume of the same title, the last published in his lifetime (1963).

* * *   (*Przeskok nad latami*), from the volume, "Spells".

p. 112   ANONYMOUS : Folklore.
THE SPARROW AND THE JACKDAW (*Ożenił się wróbel z kawką*), a peasant song from the Sandomierz district.

p. 113   I WOULD SING SONGS (*Śpiewałbym ja*), a peasant dance song.

p. 113   THE SUN SETS (*Zachodzi słoneczko*), a peasant song.

p. 113   A STONE (*Kamień na kamieniu*), a peasant song.

p. 114   NEAR MY GARDEN (*Koło mego ogródeczka*), a peasant song from the Kalisz district.

p. 115   THEY'RE NOT BIRDS (*Nie są to ptaszkowie*), a peasant song from the Poznań district.